Ninja® Foodi™ Digital Air Fry Oven
COOKBOOK FOR BEGINNERS

NINJA® Foodi™

COOKBOOK FOR BEGINNERS

75 RECIPES FOR QUICK AND EASY SHEET PAN MEALS

Janet A. Zimmerman

Photography by Becky Stayner

ROCKRIDGE
PRESS

For general information on our other products and services or to obtain technical support, please contact our Customer Care Department within the U.S. at (866) 744-2665, or outside the U.S. at (510) 253-0500.

Rockridge Press publishes its books in a variety of electronic and print formats. Some content that appears in print may not be available in electronic books, and vice versa.

TRADEMARKS: Rockridge Press and the Rockridge Press logo are trademarks or registered trademarks of Callisto Media Inc. and/or its affiliates, in the United States and other countries, and may not be used without written permission. All other trademarks are the property of their respective owners. Rockridge Press is not associated with any product or vendor mentioned in this book.

Interior and Cover Designer: Joshua Moore
Art Producer: Karen Beard
Editor: Bridget Fitzgerald
Production Editor: Andrew Yackira
Production Manager: Giraud Lorber
Photography © 2019 Becky Stayner, food styling by Kathleen Phillips and Kellie Gerber Kelley, except pp.40, 74 © Darren Muir; p. 119 © Marija Vidal & p.130 © Evi Abeler. Author photo courtesy of Court Mast, Mast Photography.

ISBN: Print 978-1-64611-017-9
eBook 978-1-64611-018-6
R0

To Dave, without whom I could never survive the process of writing a cookbook

CONTENTS

INTRODUCTION

AS MUCH AS I LOVE TO COOK, THERE HAVE BEEN STRETCHES in my life when I did precious little of it. First, when I was in, and then just out of, college, there was my lack of cooking equipment, coupled with rental kitchens and their crappy stoves. Ask me about the cheap gas stove with the broiler that randomly shot flames out—once obliterating an entire jalapeño—or the electric stove whose "Preheat" setting automatically defaulted to less time for 400ºF than it did for 200ºF.

Then there was the lack of time when I started working full-time. Weekend cooking? Fine! Weekday dinners? Not so much. Even when I had everything planned for dinner, by the time I got home, all I wanted to do was make toast, which took about all the time I had left in the day.

And I must admit to the final obstacle in my cooking life—cleanup. To this day, I hate doing dishes. I'm lucky now to have a partner who cleans up after me in the kitchen (I do the laundry and vacuuming, so it evens out). But for much of my life, whatever kitchen messes I created I had to undo. I'd make what I thought was a simple dinner, and then look around at the skillet, and the saucepan, and the baking dish, and the stack of bowls—not to mention the spattered stovetop—and think, *Who made this mess? And who's going to clean it up?*

It turns out that all I needed during those years was the Ninja® Foodi™ Digital Air Fry Oven. Except it hadn't yet been invented. But if it were around back then, it would have solved almost all my cooking woes. It's a precise, reliable oven that does everything my cheap rental ovens wouldn't—and it fits on the counter. It preheats in about a minute, and on air roast it cooks about 60 percent faster than a traditional full-size oven. It cleans up easily—the back opens, so I can wipe it down in a flash. It even flips up and folds away against my backsplash when I'm not using it, so it wouldn't have taken up

all the counter space I had back in those small apartment kitchens. It doesn't require much extra equipment—I can make complete dinners, even for company, all with little more than its generous (and delightfully nonstick) sheet pan. And, of course, it also air-fries to perfection.

If you are like that younger me, you will love this oven. The current me thinks it's amazing.

Most of us want the same things when it comes to cooking meals—we want them to be delicious, we want them to be fast, we want them to be simple, and we'd like them to be healthy. Let's face it: most of us are lucky to hit two of the four on any given day. The fastest meals are often unhealthy, and tasty food is rarely as simple as we'd like.

I'm not going to promise that the Ninja® Foodi™ Digital Air Fry Oven is going to change your life. But it will increase your odds of making those fast, tasty, simple, and healthy meals every day. Together with this book, the oven will make it possible to create a wide variety of great meals that your family will love. You can make healthier versions of your takeout favorites, from pizza to burgers to tacos. You'll be able to explore different cuisines—Chinese American beef and broccoli one day, chicken shawarma the next, Thai-inspired vegetables the third. And best of all, you can make almost all these recipes in about 30 minutes. But wait! There's more! You can make them on one sheet pan. There's no sinkful of dirty dishes to face afterward.

Quick, delicious meals. Fast, easy cleanup. With all the free time you'll have, maybe the Foodi Oven *will* change your life.

Roasted Portobellos with Peppers and Fontina, *page 89*

1

Ninja® Foodi™ Digital Air Fry Oven 101

MORE THAN EVER BEFORE, TODAY'S HOME COOKS HAVE fallen in love with a new category of kitchen appliances: those that can perform a multitude of tasks. Whether it's a slow cooker that can also pressure cook, or a pressure cooker that can also air fry (like the original Ninja® Foodi™ Pressure Cooker), these countertop wonders are changing the way we cook.

Toaster ovens have never quite achieved that rock-star status. Sure, they're great for toasting, or simple baking jobs, or reheating pizza, but their small size makes them problematic. Make them large enough for big batches of food, and you take up valuable counter space.

Enter the Ninja® Foodi™ Digital Air Fry Oven, which is big enough to cook a complete family meal in the time it takes to have a pizza delivered. It flips up and away when not in use, so it requires hardly any counter space at all. It roasts, it bakes, it toasts, it air-fries, all with fast, even heat. It's what you've been waiting for.

SO MUCH MORE THAN AN AIR FRYER

Air fryers, with their promising ability to crisp up "fried" foods with a minimum of fat and a minimum of fuss, are gaining in popularity. But like many toaster ovens, they're small. Their baskets are deep and narrow, which makes it difficult to cook food evenly, and almost impossible to cook family-size dinners.

Combination air-fryer/countertop ovens solve those issues, but instead of being small in size, most are big and bulky, which presents another set of problems. They're awkward to move and hard to store when not in use. And many kitchens lack the space to make them permanent countertop fixtures.

The Ninja® Foodi™ Digital Air Fry Oven gives you the best of both worlds—it provides lots of space to cook for your family, and flips up and away when not in use. It has a removable crumb tray and an accessible back panel for easy, thorough cleaning. With a range of cooking functions and temperatures, it can handle everything from breakfast bagels, to french fries, to a family-size sheet pan meal, to a delicate dessert.

Fast, Even Heating

The Ninja Foodi Digital Air Fry Oven preheats in about 60 seconds. Compare that with the 10 to 15 minutes a conventional oven takes to heat up, or even the five minutes a small toaster oven or air fryer takes, and you'll start to see how fast you can have dinner on the table.

Shorter Cook Times

On the Air Fry, Air Roast, and Air Broil settings, the Ninja Foodi Digital Air Fry Oven will cook faster than a conventional oven—the convection fan can speed up cooking by up to 60 percent—which makes weeknight dinners even faster.

Large Cooking Area

The square sheet pan and the air fry basket measure approximately 13 by 13 inches. That's about one-and-a-half times the size of some small toaster ovens. You can easily cook a full meal for four, or party food for a crowd, without having to cook multiple batches. The sheet pan can hold nine slices of bread at once. Nine!

Easy Cleaning

The sheet pan and air fry basket are both dishwasher safe, and the whole oven is a breeze to keep clean. The crumb tray slides out easily. The back opens for complete access to the oven, and a quick wipe down with soap and water is all it needs. The brushed stainless exterior cleans up with a damp sponge.

Convenient Storage

While the cooking surface is family-size, it won't take over your kitchen counter. That's because when it's not in use, it flips up and away, taking up 50 percent less space when folded up. Its sleek design looks great with any style of kitchen, so you'll never have to worry about using cabinet space to store it.

HOW IT WORKS

The Ninja® Foodi™ Digital Air Fry Oven is easy and intuitive to use. Just one dial controls the cooking process. First, use it to select the cooking function, then set the time and temperature (or toasting level). With a final press of the dial, the cooking process begins. It'll even pause the timer and cooking if you need to stir or add ingredients.

The oven can switch between Fahrenheit and Celsius, and it lets you know when it's preheating and when it's cool enough to clean or flip for storage. It's easy to read the timer and the temperature display (or the number of slices and darkness level for toast and bagels). Both the time and temperature default to the settings you last used.

The Control Panel

On the control panel, you'll see the time and temperature display. In the Toast or Bagel modes, you'll see number of slices and darkness level instead of time and temperature. Icons indicate when the unit is preheating, when it is hot, and whether the oven is set to Fahrenheit or Celsius. The selected function lights up under Crisp Control when the oven is turned on. The time display reads FLIP when the unit is cool enough to flip up for storage.

Under the function settings is the multifunctional dial, which starts and pauses the oven and adjusts the time and temperature (or number of slices and darkness level for toast). The Time button starts and completes setting the time (or number of toast slices), and the Temperature button does the same for temperature (or darkness level for toast). The oven light and OFF/ON button are at the bottom of the control panel.

Air Fry

Air Fry is the best choice when you want to mimic shallow or deep frying to achieve a beautiful crisp exterior, as in the Chicken Parm Sandwiches on Ciabatta (page 128) or the Crispy Bean and Cheese Tacos (page 83). The Air Fry setting uses the maximum convection fan speed and high heat from the top and bottom elements. The time can be set up to 1 hour and the temperature adjusted from 250ºF to 450ºF.

Air Roast

Air Roast is the setting I use most often for all kinds of sheet pan recipes, from Steak Fajitas (page 155) to Oven-Roasted Shrimp "Boil" (page 99) to Paprika Chicken Thighs with Toasted Slaw (page 131). The Air Roast setting uses medium convection fan speed, and even heat from the top and bottom elements. The time can be set up to 2 hours and the temperature adjusted from 250ºF to 450ºF.

Air Broil

The Air Broil setting uses medium convection fan speed and high heat from the top element. The time can be set up to 30 minutes and the temperature set to HIGH or LOW. It's useful for browning chops, steaks, or chicken or fish fillets, as in Chicken Shawarma with Roasted Tomatoes (page 144) or the Tandoori Lamb Chops (page 177).

Bake

The Bake setting uses no fan, and even heat from the top and bottom elements. The time can be set up to 2 hours and temperature adjusted from 250°F to 450°F. This setting is great for more delicate dishes like the Spiced Apple Turnovers (page 29) or Caramel Pear Tart (page 191). It's also very useful for warming tortillas for tacos or pita breads for sandwiches.

Toast

The Toast setting uses no fan, and even heat from the top and bottom elements. The Ninja® Foodi™ Digital Air Fry Oven can toast up to nine slices of bread at once. The number of slices can be set up to nine. The time is determined automatically by the number of slices, and instead of adjusting the temperature, you just tell the oven how light or dark you want your toast. It's as easy and no fuss as it gets. No more guessing for how long bread will take to toast, or hovering over the oven to make sure the toast doesn't burn.

Bagel

The Bagel setting uses no fan, and slightly lower heat from the top than from the bottom element. The Ninja Foodi Digital Air Fry Oven will toast up to six bagel slices. As with the Toast function, there is no temperature adjustment, and the time is determined automatically by the number of slices being toasted.

Using the Ninja® Foodi™ Digital Air Fry Oven

For the Air Fry, Air Roast, Air Broil, and Bake functions:

- To start the cooking process, use the dial to select the function you want. The default time and temperature setting will display. The oven will also remember your last time and temperature that was used—great for favorite recipes so you don't have to reset every time.

- To adjust the time, press the TIME/SLICE button and use the dial to change it. Press the TIME/SLICE button again to set the time.
- To set the temperature, press the TEMP/DARKNESS button and turn the dial to your recipe's temperature. Press the TEMP/DARK-NESS button again to set the temperature.
- Place your food on the sheet pan or in the Air Fry basket and slide the pan or basket in the oven. Press START/PAUSE to begin cooking.

For the Toast or Bagel functions:

- To start the toasting process, use the dial to select the function you want. The default number of slices and darkness level will display, and the oven will remember your most recently used settings for maximum efficiency in the morning.
- Place your bread or bagels, cut-side up, on the rack. (You can also do this after setting the slices and darkness level.)
- To adjust the number of slices, press the TIME/SLICE button and use the dial to change it. Press the TIME/SLICE button again to set the number of slices.
- To adjust how dark you want your toast or bagels, press the TEMP/DARKNESS button and turn the dial to your desired level. Press the TEMP/DARKNESS button again to set the level.
- Press START/PAUSE to begin toasting.

How to Convert
Conventional Oven Recipes

If you're used to a conventional oven, it can take some work to adjust your favorite recipes to a smaller, more powerful convection oven like the Ninja® Foodi™ Digital Air Fry Oven, but there are a couple of rules that can help you out.

If you're using the Bake function, which doesn't use the fan, you can often use your conventional oven recipes as is. To be on the safe side, check your food about three-quarters of the way through the original cooking time. You can always cook it longer. You may find that the proximity of the lower heating element will brown your tarts or cinnamon rolls a bit faster than a larger, conventional oven. If that seems to be happening, try reducing the temperature slightly.

For the Air Roast function, which uses the convection fan, it's recommended to lower the temperature by 25°F and decrease the cooking time by 25 to 30 percent. For instance, we cook wings in our big oven at 400°F for 35 to 40 minutes. In the Ninja Foodi Digital Air Fry Oven, I set the temperature to 375°F and cook them for about 25 minutes.

For recipes that use Air Broil, it's a bit trickier. Broilers in conventional ovens can vary so widely in heat and intensity that the wisest course of action is to keep a close eye on whatever you're broiling, and make notes to follow the next time you cook your recipe. If you're worried, use Air Broil set to LOW. You can always turn it up, but once you've overcooked your steak or fish, there's nothing you can do but add a lot of sauce.

Regardless of the Ninja Foodi Digital Air Fry Oven setting you use, always make note of the time and temperature changes you make to a conventional oven recipe so you know what to use the next time, and the next time, and the next time . . .

FREQUENTLY ASKED QUESTIONS

Q: Can I use cookware other than the accessories that come with the Ninja® Foodi™ Digital Air Fry Oven?

A: You can certainly use other sheet pans, although a standard half sheet pan will not fit. A quarter sheet pan or anything smaller will fit. (The great thing about the Ninja sheet pan is that it optimizes surface area since it's designed specifically for the Ninja Foodi Digital Air Fry Oven.) A 6-cup muffin tin will fit, as will baking pans up to 13 inches. Ovenproof ceramic baking dishes can be used, so long as they are not too deep. Because the heating elements are so close to the rack, avoid anything that is labeled not safe for a broiler.

Q: Your recipes never call for prepping ingredients while the oven heats up. Why is that?

A: Because the Ninja® Foodi™ Digital Air Fry Oven preheats so quickly! Unlike a conventional oven, which can take 10 to 15 minutes to preheat, the Ninja Foodi Digital Air Fry Oven takes about 1 minute depending on the setting. I sometimes start the oven and use the minute to transfer food to the sheet pan, but that's about all I have time for. If the oven is at temperature and the timer starts to count down, but you're not ready to insert the sheet pan, don't worry. You can adjust the time when the oven is on just by pressing "Time" and turning the dial.

Q: Why do your recipes always seem to call for tossing ingredients with sauce or seasonings in a bowl? Wouldn't I save a dirty bowl if I mixed ingredients right on the sheet pan?

A: In some cases, tossing ingredients with oil and spices is easy to do right on the sheet pan. But with larger amounts of ingredients and sauces, the rim of the sheet pan is low enough that it can be messier and more time consuming to try to mix on the pan than it is to use a bowl.

Q: Is it okay to cover the sheet pan with aluminum foil to make cleanup easier?

A: The owner's manual says not to, because the foil can trap melted fat, which can flare up. And trust me, no one wants a kitchen fire. But the sheet pan is nonstick and easy to clean, so it's really not necessary.

Q: Do I have to do anything special to fold up the oven when I'm ready to store it?

A: Make sure the back of the unit is about five inches from the wall. Then just wait for it to cool. The oven, if it is on, will display FLIP when it's cool enough. There aren't any levers or buttons to push to fold the Ninja Foodi Digital Air Fry Oven, and you don't have to do anything to lock it in place. It won't fall down. You can fold it up with the rack and air fry basket in place. Even the sheet pan will be held in place, if you want to store it in the oven.

Braised Pork Chops with Squash and Apples, *page 164*

2

Sheet Pan Magic

THE NINJA® FOODI™ DIGITAL AIR FRY OVEN CAN DO JUST about everything (except clean your kitchen for you). It'll make toast for breakfast, air fry snacks, and bake desserts. But its main advantage, especially compared with other countertop ovens, is its ability to handle big batches of food on the extra-large sheet pan. With the Ninja Foodi Digital Air Fry Oven, it's fast and easy to make appetizers for a crowd, or family dinners, breakfasts, or desserts.

Imagine cooking granola or hash and eggs in the morning, crispy tacos for lunch, salmon with asparagus for dinner, and a fruit tart for dessert. Or throwing a Super Bowl party with Crispy Lemon-Pepper Wings (page 55), Roasted Jalapeño Poppers (page 47), Pimento Cheese–Stuffed Mushrooms (page 49), and Chiles Rellenos–Style Nachos (page 65). Or showing up at your company potluck with a big batch of Oatmeal Chocolate Chip Cookie Bars (page 185). And now imagine doing it all in one countertop appliance, with only one pan. With the Ninja Foodi Digital Air Fry Oven, it's that easy, and fast, too.

And with only one pan and no dirty stove and oven to scrub, you won't mind that it can't clean your kitchen.

THE MAGIC OF THE SHEET PAN

Once upon a time, sheet pans were for baking cookies, roasting vegetables, or—if you had a rack—broiling fish or steaks. Their versatility is well-known, and it seems that everyone is jumping on the sheet pan bandwagon. And it's no wonder.

Not only can you roast vegetables, from potatoes to beets to broccoli, but you can cook just about any meat or fish, and even tofu. As you become familiar with the Ninja® Foodi™ Digital Air Fry Oven, you can combine proteins and vegetables with sauces and spice rubs to develop your own signature meals. And why stop with dinners? Delicious breakfasts, snacks, and desserts are equally easy to prepare on this ever-so-handy pan. What can't it do? You might be on your own for salads—although I even include recipes for a few warm salads made with roasted ingredients, just to prove that nothing is impossible.

A Full Meal on One Pan

One of the great things about cooking on a sheet pan is that you can cook a whole dinner on the pan, either all together, or by adding ingredients in stages. Family dinners from Curried Chicken and Sweet Potatoes (page 139) to a Snapper Veracruz (page 115), from Spicy Pork Lettuce Cups (page 161) to Beef and Crispy Broccoli (page 157), can be cooked entirely on one pan. Desserts, appetizers, and breakfasts too can be sheet pan meals. And once you are accustomed to sheet pan cooking in the Ninja Foodi Digital Air Fry Oven, you'll be custom designing your own meals by mixing and matching your favorite ingredients.

Hands-Off Cooking

In many of this book's recipes, once you slide the sheet pan into the oven, there's very little else to do but set the table. Stirring or adding ingredients takes only a few minutes, so you're not tethered to the stovetop before dinner is ready. While some of the appetizer recipes are a bit more involved, much of that work can be done in advance, so you're free to make a drink and relax while the Ninja® Foodi™ Digital Air Fry Oven does the work.

30-Minute Weeknight Cooking

Not only can you cook a wide variety of meals, snacks, and desserts using just the sheet pan, but with the Ninja Foodi Digital Air Fry Oven, cooking is as fast as it is simple. The Foodi Oven preheats in about a minute, so there's no waiting for a full-size oven to heat. And the power of the convection fan cuts most cooking times by more than 25 percent. The dinner recipes in this book mostly take 30 minutes or less—sometimes a little more, but not often.

Of course, if you have the time and inclination, you can also choose ingredients that take a little longer—ribs, for instance, or baked potatoes. It's up to you!

Easy Cleanup

What's better than a quick weeknight dinner? Quick weeknight cleanup! Since your whole meal is prepared on one pan, cleanup is a snap. The Ninja sheet pan is nonstick and dishwasher safe, so it's a breeze to wash. For most of the recipes in this book, the only other dirty dishes will be one or two bowls and a spoon or spatula.

The oven itself is also easy to clean. The crumb tray, which protects the bottom of the oven from spills, slides out for washing. The back of the oven opens completely, so you can clean all of the surfaces with just warm water and dish soap. The outside wipes clean with a sponge, and then the whole unit flips up for storage.

EQUIPPING YOUR KITCHEN

Cooking is always easier if your kitchen is adequately stocked. That doesn't mean you need every pan and gadget from the cookware store, and it doesn't mean you need a shelf filled with a dozen varieties of vinegar, or a spice rack like mine (what can I say? I have an obsession). It does mean that if you have a few basic pieces of

Sheet Pan Formulas

I write recipes for a living, but I know there are many cooks out there who'd rather wing it than follow a cookbook. The Ninja® Foodi™ Digital Air Fry Oven and its sheet pan are perfect for that kind of cook. With a few tips to get started and a little practice, you can easily create your own specialties.

Determine the Cooking Times

The first step is to figure out the cooking times for your desired ingredients. You can almost always adjust the amount of time a meal takes to cook by the size you cut your ingredients—smaller pieces cook faster. Strips of steak for fajitas will take less time to cook than a whole steak, for instance.

The second step is to match foods that cook in the same time. That's why fajitas work so well in the Ninja Foodi Digital Air Fry Oven—steak or chicken strips cook at the same rate as bell pepper strips. Snow peas are a good match for shrimp. Bone-in chicken thighs take longer, and so do roasted potatoes, so they make a good combination. Of course, with practice, you can expand your combinations by starting out with longer-cooking foods and adding the others later in the cooking process.

Season your ingredients, and that's about it. Sure, you can get fancier, but this is a good starting point.

Choose Tender Cuts

The best meat choices for sheet pan dinners are the tender cuts—pork tenderloin, boneless chicken breasts or thighs, or one of the beef steak cuts. Any fish or shellfish will work, as will firm tofu. For quick cooking, slice your beef or pork tenderloin and cut chicken into chunks. If you have more time, you can leave the meat in larger pieces.

Pick the Right Vegetables

Vegetables fall into two main categories for roasting. Dense vegetables like sweet potatoes, squash, potatoes, and beets will take longer than asparagus, green beans, or sugar snap peas. Although, as mentioned previously, you can decrease the cooking time of the denser vegetables by cutting them smaller. Peppers, carrots, and onions can go both ways—cut them into thin strips or dice, and they'll cook quickly. Cut them into large wedges or chunks, and they'll stand up to longer cooking.

Season to Taste

For easy seasoning, spice blends work well, as do commercially prepared sauces like teriyaki or curry pastes. If you use a spice blend, toss the ingredients with a touch of oil or butter before seasoning—not only will the spices adhere better, but the oil protects and browns your ingredients. Pay attention to the salt level of your seasonings; I use mostly salt-free mixtures, so I add my own salt. But most commercial blends contain salt, so skip the salt at first and season to taste later.

Adjust as Needed

If your proteins are sliced or cut into chunks (or for fish, thin fillets) and you choose quick-cooking vegetables, count on 12 to 15 minutes of cooking time. For larger pieces of meat and longer-cooking vegetables, 17 to 20 minutes will probably suffice. Always check your ingredients during cooking so you don't overcook them. You can always cook them longer!

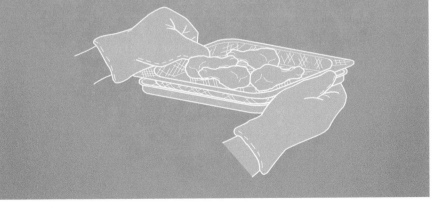

cookware, essential utensils, and pantry staples, it'll be more pleasant and less stressful when you walk into the kitchen and open your cookbook.

Go-To Staples

It's hard to tell cooks how to stock their pantries. So much depends on your personal preferences—not only your own likes and dislikes, but also the types of cuisines you like. I like a wide variety, and my recipes reflect that. So, here's a really long list of things I use. Don't buy them all at once; look through the recipes first to see what appeals to you, and adjust your shopping list accordingly.

Oils: Extra-virgin olive oil is nice when you want a distinct flavor. Vegetable oil and grapeseed oil are more neutral. Toasted sesame oil is a must if you want to cook Asian dishes. You'll also want a basic cooking oil spray.

Vinegars: You should have either red or white wine vinegar on hand. If you like Asian-style cuisines, rice vinegar (unseasoned) is crucial. For extra-special dishes, I like to have aged sherry vinegar or aged balsamic (or both) in my cabinet. For the balsamic, look for Villa Manodori. It's not cheap, but it's less expensive than comparable brands, and it lasts forever.

Hot sauces: I regularly keep two types on hand—either Tabasco or Crystal, and sriracha or Asian chili-garlic paste.

Other condiments: Dijon mustard and mayonnaise are staples in my pantry.

Canned goods: Canned beans, jars of roasted red peppers, and cans of diced tomatoes are good to have on hand. I also often use capers, because my adorable, otherwise perfect partner does not like pickles, and capers are a compromise I can live with. You can probably do without them, but they do show up in some recipes.

Stock: For recipes that call for chicken or vegetable stock, choose a low-sodium stock, or reduce the amount of salt in the recipe by about a third.

One thing that can speed up dinner prep and still result in tasty meals is the judicious use of commercial sauces. I say "judicious" because some of what's out there is not great. But here are some that I use in my recipes:

Marinara sauce: When I don't have the time to make my own (page 195), I use Classico Riserva Marinara. They also make a very good Arrabiata, if you like things spicy.

Salsa: Frontera brand Double Roasted Tomato and Tomatillo salsas are almost as good as my own, and I don't say that lightly.

Teriyaki sauce: I generally make my own (page 199), but I've heard very good things about Trader Joe's Soyaki sauce. Kikkoman also has a good variety of teriyaki sauces.

Hoisin and soy sauces: I know there are products out there called "stir-fry sauce," but I tend to make mine from scratch for stir-fries and stir-fry-like dishes (see Asian-Style Sauce, page 197). You'll want Hoisin sauce and soy sauce (I use Pearl River brand) to make that, and those aren't bad things to have on hand, even if you don't make my recipe.

Freezer goods: Frozen ingredients that appear in my recipes include corn, artichoke hearts, spinach, and peas. I have found Dorot brand frozen minced ginger and garlic cubes to be a game changer. While there are jars and tubes of garlic and ginger purée available, I've never much liked them. For desserts and breakfast items, I use frozen puff pastry often.

Fridge items: From the fridge, you'll want eggs, unsalted butter, heavy (whipping) cream, milk, pizza dough, and rolled piecrusts. These are more common in breakfast and dessert recipes, but they do make appearances elsewhere.

Cheeses: I love cheese. While I do develop recipes without cheese, many of the recipes in this book call for sharp cheddar, mozzarella, Monterey Jack, or Swiss-style cheeses. Ricotta makes an appearance or two. In most cases, buying blocks of cheese and grating it yourself is cheaper and gives better results. But Sargento has some good-quality shredded cheeses, so if you want to go that way, check out that brand.

One cheese you should invest in is what is popularly called Parmesan. The "real" Parm is Parmigiano Reggiano. It's fabulous, but these days there are some pretty good domestic versions that will work fine for these recipes. Sartori SarVecchio is a good choice, and Trader Joe's sells a good version as well. You can also look for Grana Padano, which used to be much cheaper than true Parm, although that price gap has mostly closed.

Go-To Spice Rack

If there's anything harder to compile than a pantry list, it's a list of spices for your rack. I believe in lots of spices. I don't expect everyone to be like me, so do what works for you. Here are the herbs and spices I use most often in this book:

Dried herbs: Thyme, oregano, and basil. An Italian herb mixture is nice, too.

Spices: Cinnamon, cayenne pepper, cumin, red pepper flakes, curry powder (I like Penzey's Hot blend), chili powder (I use Penzey's blend without salt). Smoked paprika is a great addition to the spice rack, and fortunately, it has become more widely available. If you can't find it, regular sweet (not hot) paprika makes an acceptable substitute.

Spice mixtures: As with commercial sauces, spice mixtures can be a great way to cut down on dinner prep time. As is probably no surprise, I make most of my own blends, and I've included some in recipes, where appropriate. The one I use most often is a Southwestern Seasoning (page 206). Fajita seasoning can be used instead, but those can be wildly unpredictable.

Salt and pepper: With very few exceptions, I use Diamond brand kosher salt in my recipes, but I've specified amounts for fine salt as well (half the amount, in general). Finally, I call for freshly ground black pepper. Pre-ground black pepper loses its flavor so fast, it's hardly worth using.

Go-To Tools and Accessories

Another advantage to cooking with the Ninja® Foodi™ Digital Air Fry Oven is that you won't need a cabinet full of equipment. For most of the recipes, you'll only need the sheet pan once you start cooking. A couple of the recipes use the Air Fry basket, and some of the Staples recipes use a baking pan. But that's it. No pots and pans, no skillets. You may want to order a second sheet pan from Ninja so you'll have a backup, but that's optional.

Timer: I find that an extra timer is really helpful for those times when I have to check a dish halfway through to turn or toss ingredients. That way, I can set the Ninja Foodi Digital Air Fry Oven for the total time and not have to reset it.

Meat thermometer: When you start using a new appliance, you may find that your usual recipes don't cook at the same rate. It's best to be safe when it comes to cooking chicken thighs or pork chops and check their internal temperature during cooking.

Oil mister/sprayer: I call for cooking oil spray in some recipes, and while you can use a store-bought spray, I know that some cooks prefer to use their own oil in a spray bottle.

Prep tools: For prep, you'll need a cutting board and knives, and a few bowls—small ones for sauces, larger ones for mixing ingredients. Other necessary tools include whisks and spoons for stirring and spatulas and tongs for moving food around. Of course, you'll need sturdy, thick pot holders or oven mitts for getting the hot sheet pan out of the oven.

ABOUT THE RECIPES

The recipes in this book are mostly divided by the main ingredient, except for three course-driven chapters—Breakfast, Snacks and Appetizers, and Desserts and Staples. They're flagged with several labels, so you can easily choose meals that meet your dietary requirements, cooking style, and tastes:

- Dairy-free
- Gluten-free
- Nut-free
- Vegetarian or Vegan
- Family Favorite
- 5-Ingredient
- Under 30 Minutes

At the beginning of each recipe, there's an "at a glance" line that indicates prep time, cooking time, and the total time. In most cases, the total time is under 30 minutes, with some recipes taking an extra 5 to 10 minutes. A few of the recipes benefit from extra time for such things as chilling dough or marinating meat, but as these steps are not absolutely necessary, those times are not included in the total.

I've tried to be as accurate as possible, but the times can vary depending on many factors. The size, temperature, or age of ingredients can affect cooking times. (Large chicken thighs will take longer than small ones; eggs straight from the fridge may cook more slowly than ones that have been sitting at room temperature.) I'll always include a note about how the finished dish should look, so use those notes as a guide, rather than depending solely on the given times.

Also at the beginning of each recipe is a short introduction that may contain important information about the ingredients or instructions for the recipe. Please don't skip reading them; you might miss something crucial.

Almost all the recipes in this book use only the Ninja® Foodi™ Digital Air Fry Oven sheet pan; for those few that use other accessories, they will be noted.

The recipes also contain nutritional information. The entrée recipes in this book make four to six servings; most of the appetizer and snack recipes make more. For main dishes, the serving sizes are generous; if you have smaller appetites, they might yield more than the specified number of servings. If you're serving hungry teenagers, all bets are off.

Some of the recipes are followed by tips, which may include alternate ingredients, information about unusual ingredients or techniques, time-saving steps, or variations. Finally, some recipes call for commercial sauces or spice mixtures; in most of those cases, I provide directions for making your own from scratch, just in case you like that sort of thing.

As much as possible, I've chosen recipes that are fast and fairly simple to make. Generally, they call for fewer than ten ingredients, all of which can be found in most grocery stores. Finally, I've tried to include a mix of different styles and cuisines in the book, so I hope you'll find a variety of dishes that appeal to you. Now, let's cook!

Classic Corned Beef Hash and Eggs, *page 31*

3

Breakfast

Eggs Florentine

I first had eggs Florentine when I was a teenager, at a fancy restaurant for brunch. I'm a big fan of spinach, so I was hooked on the combination of creamy spinach with soft-cooked eggs. It's easy to make at home when you start with frozen spinach; just make sure to drain it well before mixing it with the other ingredients.

NUT-FREE, GLUTEN-FREE, VEGETARIAN, UNDER 30 MINUTES

PREP TIME: 10 minutes
AIR ROAST: 12 minutes
TOTAL TIME: 27 minutes

DID YOU KNOW:
"Florentine" in culinary circles just means a dish made with spinach, usually mixed with cream and seasonings.

- **3 cups frozen spinach, thawed and drained**
- **¼ teaspoon kosher salt or ⅛ teaspoon fine salt**
- **4 ounces ricotta cheese**
- **2 tablespoons heavy (whipping) cream**
- **2 garlic cloves, minced**
- **⅛ teaspoon freshly ground white or black pepper**
- **2 teaspoons unsalted butter, melted**
- **3 tablespoons grated Parmesan or similar cheese**
- **½ cup panko bread crumbs**
- **4 large eggs**

1. In a medium bowl, stir together the spinach, salt, ricotta, cream, garlic, and pepper.

2. In a small bowl, stir together the butter, cheese, and panko. Set aside.

3. Scoop the spinach mixture into four even circles on the sheet pan.

4. Select AIR ROAST, set temperature to 375°F, and set time to 15 minutes. Select START/PAUSE to begin preheating.

5. Once the unit has preheated, slide the sheet pan into the oven.

CONTINUED ▶

6. After 8 minutes, press PAUSE and remove the pan. The spinach should be bubbling. With the back of a large spoon, make indentations in the spinach for the eggs. Crack the eggs into the indentations and sprinkle the panko mixture over the surface of the eggs.

7. Return the pan to the oven and press START to resume cooking. After 5 minutes, check the eggs. If the eggs are done to your liking, remove the pan. If not, continue cooking.

8. When cooking is complete, remove the pan from the oven. Serve the eggs with toasted English muffins, if desired.

Per serving: *Calories: 241; Total Fat: 14g; Saturated Fat: 7g; Cholesterol: 216mg; Sodium: 263mg; Carbohydrates: 15g; Fiber: 3g; Protein: 13g*

Blueberry Sheet Pan Cake

SERVES 8

Cross a pancake with blueberry muffins and you'll get this easy, delicious break-fast treat. If you're in the mood for pancakes, simply cut and serve with butter and your favorite syrup. Or, if muffins are what you crave, brush the tops with butter and sprinkle with confectioners' sugar. You can even do both!

NUT-FREE, VEGETARIAN, FAMILY FAVORITE, UNDER 30 MINUTES

PREP TIME: 8 minutes
BAKE: 10 minutes
TOTAL TIME: 18 minutes

1½ cups Bisquick or similar baking mix

¼ cup granulated sugar (use ⅓ cup for a sweeter cake)

¾ cup whole milk

2 large eggs

1 teaspoon vanilla extract

½ teaspoon lemon zest (optional)

Cooking oil spray

2 cups blueberries

1 tablespoon butter, melted (optional)

½ cup syrup (optional)

2 tablespoons confectioners' sugar (optional)

1. In a medium bowl, whisk together the baking mix and sugar. In a small bowl, whisk together the milk, eggs, vanilla, and lemon zest (if using). Add the wet ingredients to the dry ingredients and stir just until combined (the mixture will be a little bit lumpy).

2. Spray the sheet pan with cooking oil spray, then place a square of parchment paper on the sheet, pressing it into place. Spray the parchment with cooking oil spray. Pour the batter into the pan and spread it out evenly. (It's okay if it doesn't go all the way into the corners; it will spread.) Sprinkle the blueberries evenly over the top.

3. Select BAKE, set temperature to 375ºF, and set time to 10 minutes. Select START/PAUSE to begin preheating

4. Once the unit has preheated, slide the sheet pan into the oven.

CONTINUED ▶

5. When cooking is complete, the pan cake should be pulling away from the edges of the pan and the top should be just starting to turn golden brown.

6. If serving as pancakes, let the cake cool for a minute, then cut into 16 squares and serve with butter and syrup.

7. If serving as "muffins," brush the top of the cake with the melted butter. Let the cake cool for 3 to 4 minutes, then dust with the confectioners' sugar. Slice and serve.

Per serving: Calories: 174; Total Fat: 6g; Saturated Fat: 2g; Cholesterol: 49mg; Sodium: 314mg; Carbohydrates: 27g; Fiber: 1g; Protein: 4g

Spiced Apple Turnovers

SERVES 4

If you've never made apple turnovers from scratch, you're in for a treat. They're surprisingly easy if you start with ready-made puff pastry. For an even quicker breakfast, make the filling and form the pastries the night before. Cover and refrigerate, then in the morning finish them with the egg wash and a sprinkle of sugar and bake. I like my turnovers on the tart side; if you prefer a sweeter filling, increase the brown sugar by a teaspoon or two.

NUT-FREE, VEGETARIAN, FAMILY FAVORITE

PREP TIME: 15 minutes
BAKE: 20 minutes
TOTAL TIME: 35 minutes

VARIATION: For a savory turnover, fill the pastry with scrambled eggs, shredded cheese, and bacon or sausage (¼ to ⅓ cup total filling).

HACK IT: If you're pressed for time, you can use canned apple pie filling.

1 cup diced apple (about 1 medium apple)

1 tablespoon brown sugar

¼ teaspoon cinnamon

⅛ teaspoon allspice

1 teaspoon freshly squeezed lemon juice

1 teaspoon all-purpose flour, plus more for dusting

½ package (1 sheet) frozen puff pastry, thawed

1 large egg, beaten

2 teaspoons granulated sugar

1. In a medium bowl, stir together the apple, brown sugar, cinnamon, allspice, lemon juice, and flour.

2. Lightly flour a cutting board. Unfold the puff pastry sheet onto the board. Using a rolling pin, gently roll the dough to smooth out the folds, seal any tears, and form it into a square. Cut the dough into four squares.

3. Scoop a quarter of the apple mixture into the center of each puff pastry square and spread it evenly in a triangle shape over half the pastry, leaving a border of about ½ inch around the edges of the pastry. Fold the pastry diagonally over the filling to form triangles. With a fork, crimp the edges to seal them. Place the turnovers on the sheet pan, spacing them evenly.

4. Cut two or three small slits in the top of each turnover. Brush with the egg. Sprinkle evenly with the granulated sugar.

CONTINUED ▶

5. Select BAKE, set temperature to 350°F, and set time to 20 minutes. Select START/PAUSE to begin preheating.

6. Once the unit has preheated, slide the sheet pan into the oven.

7. After 10 to 12 minutes, remove the pan from the oven. Check the pastries; if they are browning unevenly, rotate the pan. Return the pan to the oven and continue cooking.

8. When cooking is complete, remove the pan from the oven. The turnovers should be golden brown and the filling bubbling. Let cool for about 10 minutes before serving (the filling will be very hot).

Per serving: *Calories: 399; Total Fat: 24g; Saturated Fat: 6g; Cholesterol: 47mg; Sodium: 170mg; Carbohydrates: 40g; Fiber: 2g; Protein: 6g*

Classic Corned Beef Hash and Eggs

I used to wait until after St. Patrick's Day to make corned beef hash with leftovers, until I realized that you can buy thick slices of cooked corned beef at the deli counter and use that. Now I can make it whenever I want. Feel free to substitute leftover cooked roast beef, steak, or even pork chops in place of the corned beef.

DAIRY-FREE, NUT-FREE, GLUTEN-FREE, UNDER 30 MINUTES

PREP TIME: 10 minutes
AIR ROAST: 12 minutes
TOTAL TIME: 27 minutes

VARIATION: If you like your hash more cohesive, use a large fork to lightly smash the potatoes before adding the corned beef. Stir in ¼ cup of low-sodium chicken or vegetable stock with the corned beef.

- 2 medium Yukon Gold potatoes, peeled, cut into ¼-inch cubes (about 3 cups)
- 1 medium onion, chopped (about 1 cup)
- ⅓ cup diced red bell pepper
- 3 tablespoons vegetable oil
- ½ teaspoon dried thyme
- ½ teaspoon kosher salt or ¼ teaspoon fine salt, divided
- ½ teaspoon freshly ground black pepper, divided
- ¾ pound corned beef, cut into ¼-inch pieces
- 4 large eggs

1. In a large bowl, mix the potatoes, onion, red pepper, oil, thyme, ¼ teaspoon of salt, and ¼ teaspoon of pepper. Spread the vegetables on the sheet pan in an even layer.

2. Select AIR ROAST, set temperature to 375ºF, and set time to 25 minutes. Select START/PAUSE to begin preheating.

3. Once the unit has preheated, slide the sheet pan into the oven.

4. After 15 minutes, remove the pan from the oven and add the corned beef. Stir the mixture to incorporate the corned beef. Return the pan to the oven and continue cooking for 5 minutes.

CONTINUED ▶

5. After 5 minutes (20 minutes total), remove the pan from the oven. Using a large spoon, create 4 circles in the hash to hold the eggs. Gently crack an egg into each circle; season eggs with remaining ¼ teaspoon of salt and ¼ teaspoon of pepper. Return the sheet pan to the oven. Continue cooking for 3 to 8 minutes, depending on how you like your eggs (3 to 4 minutes for runny yolks; 8 minutes for firm yolks).

6. When cooking is complete, remove the pan from the oven. Serve immediately.

Per serving: *Calories: 397; Total Fat: 26g; Saturated Fat: 7g; Cholesterol: 239mg; Sodium: 777mg; Carbohydrates: 21g; Fiber: 3g; Protein: 20g*

Mini Cinnamon Sticky Rolls

MAKES 18 MINI ROLLS

What happens when you cross a cinnamon roll with a sticky bun, add a touch of palmier *to the mix, and then shrink them down? These delightful little pastries! Commercial puff pastry makes them easy, and the Ninja® Foodi™ Digital Air Fry Oven cooks them quickly. They also make a great after-school snack.*

NUT-FREE, FAMILY FAVORITE, VEGETARIAN, UNDER 5 INGREDIENTS

PREP TIME: 10 minutes
BAKE: 25 minutes
TOTAL TIME: 35 minutes

SUBSTITUTION: If you don't have light brown sugar, use a combination of 2 parts dark brown sugar to one part granulated sugar. You can also just use granulated sugar, although the flavor won't be quite as complex.

2 teaspoons cinnamon

⅓ cup light brown sugar

1 (9-by-9-inch) frozen puff pastry sheet, thawed

All-purpose flour, for dusting

6 teaspoons (2 tablespoons) unsalted butter, melted, divided

1. In a small bowl, mix together the cinnamon and brown sugar.

2. Unfold the puff pastry on a lightly floured surface. Using a rolling pin, press the folds together and roll the dough out in one direction so that it measures about 9 by 11 inches. Cut it in half to form two squat rectangles of about 5½ by 9 inches.

3. Brush 2 teaspoons of butter over each pastry half, and then sprinkle with 2 generous tablespoons of the cinnamon sugar. Pat it down lightly with the palm of your hand to help it adhere to the butter.

4. Starting with the 9-inch side of one rectangle and using your hands, carefully roll the dough into a cylinder. Repeat with the other rectangle. To make slicing easier, refrigerate the rolls for 10 to 20 minutes.

CONTINUED ▶

5. Using a sharp knife, slice each roll into nine 1-inch pieces. Transfer the rolls to the center of the sheet pan. They should be very close to each other, but not quite touching. For neater rolls, turn the outside rolls so that the seam is to the inside. Drizzle the remaining 2 teaspoons of butter over the rolls and sprinkle with the remaining cinnamon sugar.

6. Select BAKE, set temperature to 350°F, and set time to 25 minutes. Select START/PAUSE to begin preheating.

7. Once the unit has preheated, slide the sheet pan into the oven.

8. When cooking is complete, remove the pan and check the rolls. They should be puffed up and golden brown. If the rolls in the center are not quite done, return the pan to the oven for another 3 to 5 minutes. If the outside rolls are dark golden brown before the inside rolls are done, you can remove those with a small spatula before returning the pan to the oven.

9. Let the rolls cool for a couple of minutes, then transfer them to a rack to cool completely.

Per serving (2 rolls): *Calories: 149; Total Fat: 9g; Saturated Fat: 5g; Cholesterol: 7mg; Sodium: 94mg; Carbohydrates: 16g; Fiber: 1g; Protein: 2g*

French Toast Casserole

For French toast without the mess of frying, try a Ninja® Foodi™ Digital Air Fry Oven version. This delicious casserole is made like a bread pudding and baked until it's crisp on the outside, with a silky, creamy interior. No more messy drips on the stove!

NUT-FREE, VEGETARIAN,
UNDER 30 MINUTES

PREP TIME: 10 minutes
AIR ROAST: 12 minutes
TOTAL TIME: 22 minutes

3 large eggs

1 cup whole milk

¼ teaspoon kosher salt or
⅛ teaspoon fine salt

1 tablespoon pure
maple syrup

1 teaspoon vanilla

¼ teaspoon cinnamon

3 cups (1-inch) stale bread
cubes (3 to 4 slices)

1 tablespoon unsalted
butter, at room
temperature

1. In a medium bowl, whisk the eggs until the yolks and whites are completely mixed. Add the milk, salt, maple syrup, vanilla, and cinnamon and whisk to combine. Add the bread cubes and gently stir to coat with the egg mixture. Let sit for 2 to 3 minutes so the bread absorbs some of the custard, then gently stir again.

2. Grease the bottom of the sheet pan with the butter. Pour the bread mixture onto the pan, spreading it out evenly.

3. Select AIR ROAST, set temperature to 350°F, and set time to 12 minutes. Select START/PAUSE to begin preheating.

4. Once the unit has preheated, slide the pan into the oven.

5. After about 10 minutes, remove the pan and check the casserole. The top should be browned and the middle of the casserole just set. If more time is needed, return the pan to the oven and continue cooking.

6. When cooking is complete, serve warm with additional butter and maple syrup, if desired.

Per serving: *Calories: 211; Total Fat: 7g; Saturated Fat: 3g; Cholesterol: 102mg; Sodium: 366mg; Carbohydrates: 29g; Fiber: 1g; Protein: 10g*

Artichoke-Mushroom Frittata

A frittata is a sort of flat omelet, with the "fillings" all mixed in with the eggs. They're often started on the stove, then finished in the oven, but this recipe uses the Ninja® Foodi™ Digital Air Fry Oven from start to finish, for a mess-free, easy breakfast or lunch.

NUT-FREE, GLUTEN-FREE, VEGETARIAN, UNDER 30 MINUTES

PREP TIME: 10 minutes
AIR ROAST: 12 minutes
AIR BROIL: 3 minutes
TOTAL TIME: 25 minutes

VARIATION: Frittatas are almost endlessly versatile. You can use whatever cooked vegetables you like, add meat, or switch the cheese. Just don't use raw vegetables—they'll release too much liquid, and the eggs won't set up right.

2 tablespoons unsalted butter, melted

¼ cup chopped onion

1 cup coarsely chopped artichoke hearts (drained if canned; thawed if frozen)

8 eggs

½ teaspoon kosher salt or ¼ teaspoon fine salt

¼ cup whole milk

¾ cup shredded mozzarella cheese, divided

½ cup Oven-Roasted Mushrooms (page 201)

¼ cup grated Parmesan cheese

¼ teaspoon freshly ground black pepper

1. Brush the sheet pan with the butter. Add the onion and artichoke hearts and toss to coat with the butter.

2. Select AIR ROAST, set temperature to 375ºF, and set time to 12 minutes. Select START/PAUSE to begin preheating.

3. Once the unit has preheated, slide the pan into the oven.

4. While the vegetables cook, whisk the eggs with the salt in a medium bowl. Let sit for a minute or two, then add the milk and whisk again. The eggs should be thoroughly mixed with no streaks of white remaining, but not foamy. Stir in ½ cup of mozzarella cheese.

5. After the vegetables have cooked for 5 minutes, remove the pan. Spread the mushrooms over the vegetables. Pour the egg mixture over the vegetables. Stir gently just to distribute the vegetables evenly. Return the pan to the oven and resume cooking for 5 to 7 minutes, or until the edges are set. The center will still be quite liquid. (If the frittata begins to form large bubbles on the bottom, use a silicone spatula to break the bubbles and let the air out so the frittata flattens out again.)

6. Select AIR BROIL, set temperature to LOW, and set time to 3 minutes. Press START/PAUSE to begin. After 1 minute, remove the pan and sprinkle the remaining ¼ cup of mozzarella and the Parmesan cheese over the frittata. Return the pan to the oven and continue cooking for the remaining 2 minutes.

7. When cooking is complete, the cheese should be melted, with the top completely set but not browned. Sprinkle the black pepper over the frittata.

Per serving: Calories: 197; Total Fat: 14g; Saturated Fat: 7g; Cholesterol: 244mg; Sodium: 438mg; Carbohydrates: 4g; Fiber: 2g; Protein: 13g

Granola with Cashews

I never liked granola much, until I had it at a friend's house. When I asked where she got it, she laughed and said she'd made it. It hadn't occurred to me until then that it was something you could make at home, but it's really easy. And way better than store-bought. This granola goes great with apple slices, a handful of blueberries, or strawberries.

DAIRY-FREE, GLUTEN-FREE, VEGETARIAN, UNDER 30 MINUTES

PREP TIME: 5 minutes
BAKE: 12 minutes
TOTAL TIME: 27 minutes

- 3 cups old-fashioned rolled oats
- 2 cups raw cashews or mixed raw nuts (such as pecans, walnuts, almonds)
- 1 cup unsweetened coconut chips
- ½ cup honey
- ¼ cup vegetable oil, extra-virgin olive oil, or walnut oil
- ⅓ cup packed light brown sugar
- ¼ teaspoon kosher salt or ⅛ teaspoon fine salt
- 1 cup dried cranberries (optional)

1. Place the oats, nuts, coconut, honey, oil, brown sugar, and salt in a large bowl and mix until well combined. Spread the mixture in an even layer on the sheet pan.

2. Select BAKE, set temperature to 325ºF, and set time to 12 minutes. Select START/PAUSE to begin preheating.

3. Once the unit has preheated, slide the pan into the oven.

4. After 5 to 6 minutes, remove the pan and stir the granola, return the pan to the oven, and continue cooking.

5. When cooking is complete, remove the pan. Let the granola cool to room temperature, then stir in the cranberries, if using. If not serving right away, store in an airtight container at room temperature.

Per serving: Calories: 650; Total Fat: 34g; Saturated Fat: 9g; Cholesterol: 0mg; Sodium: 37mg; Carbohydrates: 77g; Fiber: 6g; Protein: 13g

Pepperoni Pizza Bites, *page 58*

4

Snacks and Appetizers

Mini Twice-Baked Cheesy Potatoes

SERVES 6

I've been making some version or other of these potato bites since I started teaching cooking classes 20 years ago. They're always a hit, and while they do take a bit of time to assemble, you can do that in advance and then refrigerate them for a couple of hours (or even overnight, if covered with plastic wrap) until you're ready to bake. Just increase the final cooking time so they have time to heat all the way through.

NUT-FREE, GLUTEN-FREE, VEGETARIAN

PREP TIME: 15 minutes
AIR ROAST: 20 minutes
TOTAL TIME: 35 minutes

HACK IT: If you have left-over mashed potatoes, mix them with the cheese and chives. Mix the Parmesan cheese with ¼ cup of panko bread crumbs and 1 tablespoon of melted unsalted butter. Roll the potato mixture into 1-inch balls and coat with the panko. Bake as directed, until golden brown and hot all the way through.

12 small red or yellow potatoes, about 2 inches in diameter, depending on size

1 teaspoon kosher salt or ½ teaspoon fine salt, divided

1 tablespoon extra-virgin olive oil

¼ cup grated sharp cheddar cheese

¼ cup sour cream

2 tablespoons chopped chives

2 tablespoons grated Parmesan cheese

1. Place the potatoes in a large bowl. Sprinkle with the kosher salt and drizzle with the olive oil. Toss to coat. Place the potatoes on the sheet pan. Wipe out the bowl and set aside.

2. Select AIR ROAST, set temperature to 375°F, and set time to 15 minutes. Select START/PAUSE to begin preheating.

3. Once the unit has preheated, slide the pan into the oven.

4. After 10 minutes, rotate the pan 180 degrees and continue cooking.

5. When cooking is complete, check the potatoes. A sharp knife should pierce the flesh easily; if not, cook for a few more minutes. Remove the pan and let the potatoes cool until you can handle them. Halve the potatoes lengthwise. If needed, cut a small slice from the uncut side for stability. Using a small melon baller or spoon, scoop the flesh into the bowl, leaving a thin shell of skin. Place the potato halves on the sheet pan.

6. Mash the scooped-out potatoes until smooth. Add the remaining ½ teaspoon of salt, cheddar cheese, sour cream, and chives and mix until well combined. Taste and adjust the salt, if needed. Spoon the filling into a pastry bag or heavy plastic bag with one corner snipped off. Pipe the filling into the potato shells, mounding up slightly. Sprinkle with the Parmesan cheese.

7. Select AIR ROAST, set temperature to 375ºF, and set time to 5 minutes. Select START/PAUSE to begin preheating.

8. Once the unit has preheated, slide the pan into the oven.

9. When cooking is complete, the tops should be browning slightly. If necessary, cook for a couple of minutes longer. Remove the pan from the oven and let the potatoes cool slightly before serving.

Per serving: Calories: 302; Total Fat: 7g; Saturated Fat: 3g; Cholesterol: 11mg; Sodium: 464mg; Carbohydrates: 54g; Fiber: 8g; Protein: 8g

Roasted Jalapeño Poppers

I have to admit, I love the breaded, deep-fried version of jalapeño poppers—if someone else makes them. They're delicious, but a lot of work and a big mess. This roasted version is much easier, and just as tasty. If you're frying the bacon for this recipe, use some of the bacon fat instead of the butter with the panko mixture for extra smoky flavor.

NUT-FREE, UNDER
30 MINUTES

PREP TIME: 10 minutes
AIR ROAST: 15 minutes
TOTAL TIME: 27 minutes

SUBSTITUTION: If you're serving kids or people who like their snacks on the mild side, use miniature bell peppers instead of jalapeños.

DID YOU KNOW: The heat of a jalapeño is determined, in part, by the growing conditions, which is why it's difficult to know in advance how hot your particular chiles will be. Removing the seeds and ribs will cut down on the heat.

12 large jalapeño peppers (about 3 inches long)

6 ounces cream cheese, at room temperature

1 teaspoon chili powder

4 ounces shredded cheddar cheese

2 slices cooked bacon, chopped fine

¼ cup panko bread crumbs

1 tablespoon butter, melted

1. If the jalapeños have stems, cut them off flush with the tops of the chiles. Slice the jalapeños in half lengthwise and scoop out the seeds. For milder poppers, remove the white membranes (the ribs). (You should probably wear latex gloves when you do this, to avoid possible burns. I often forget, and I often regret it.)

2. In a medium bowl, mix the cream cheese, chili powder, and cheddar cheese. Spoon the cheese mixture into the jalapeño halves and place them on the sheet pan. If the jalapeños roll or tip, use a vegetable peeler to scrape away a thin layer of skin on the base so they're more stable.

3. In a small bowl, stir together the bacon, panko, and butter. Top each of the jalapeño halves with the panko mixture.

4. Select AIR ROAST, set temperature to 375°F, and set time to 15 minutes. Select START/PAUSE to begin preheating.

CONTINUED ▶

Roasted Jalapeño Poppers continued

5. Once the unit has preheated, slide the pan into the oven.

6. After 7 or 8 minutes, rotate the pan 180 degrees and continue cooking until the peppers have softened somewhat, the filling is bubbling, and the panko is browned.

7. When cooking is complete, remove the pan from the oven. Let the poppers cool for a few minutes before serving.

Per serving: Calories: 190; Total Fat: 16g; Saturated Fat: 9g; Cholesterol: 47mg; Sodium: 299mg; Carbohydrates: 5g; Fiber: 1g; Protein: 8g

Pimento Cheese–Stuffed Mushrooms

SERVES 12

Until I moved to Atlanta, I'd never tried pimento (aka pimiento) cheese. To be honest, I wasn't quite sure what it was; I just assumed I wouldn't like it. But it turns out that when made well, it's quite tasty. In these mushrooms, I substitute cream cheese for the usual mayonnaise since it melts better. I use jarred piquillo peppers since it can be difficult to find real pimiento peppers, but any roasted red peppers will do.

NUT-FREE, VEGETARIAN

PREP TIME: 15 minutes
AIR ROAST: 12 minutes
TOTAL TIME: 32 minutes

DID YOU KNOW: If you've heard or read that you shouldn't wash mushrooms but rather brush them off or wipe them with a damp paper towel, you can ignore that advice. The reason given is that mushrooms will absorb excess water, but mushroom cells are already so full of water that it really makes no difference. I always soak my mushrooms for a few minutes in my salad spinner, swishing them around to dislodge any dirt, then lift the basket up out of the dirty water, giving me clean mushrooms with no tedious brushing.

- 24 medium raw white button or cremini mushrooms (about 1½ inches in diameter)
- 4 ounces shredded extra-sharp cheddar cheese
- 2 tablespoons grated onion
- 1 ounce chopped jarred pimientos or roasted red pepper (about ¼ cup)
- ⅛ teaspoon smoked paprika
- ⅛ teaspoon hot sauce, such as Crystal or Tabasco
- 2 ounces cream cheese, at room temperature
- 2 tablespoons butter, melted, divided
- 2 tablespoons grated Parmesan cheese
- ⅓ cup panko bread crumbs

1. Wash the mushrooms and drain. Gently pull out the stems and discard (or save for another use; they make great vegetable stock). If your mushrooms are on the small side, or you feel like some extra work, you can use a small spoon or melon baller to remove some of the gills to form a larger cavity. Set aside.

2. In a medium bowl, combine the cheddar cheese, onion, pimientos, paprika, hot sauce, and cream cheese. The mixture should be smooth with no large streaks of cream cheese visible.

3. Brush the sheet pan with 1 tablespoon of melted butter. Arrange the mushrooms evenly over the pan, hollow-side up.

CONTINUED ▶

4. Place the cheese mixture into a large heavy plastic bag and cut off the end. Fill the mushrooms with the cheese mixture.

5. In a small bowl, stir together the Parmesan, panko, and remaining 1 tablespoon of melted butter. Sprinkle a little of the panko mixture over each mushroom (or carefully dip the filled tops of the mushrooms into the mixture to coat).

6. Select AIR ROAST, set temperature to 350°F, and set time to 18 minutes. Select START/PAUSE to begin preheating.

7. Once the unit has preheated, slide the pan into the oven.

8. After about 9 minutes, rotate the pan 180 degrees and continue cooking.

9. When cooking is complete, let the stuffed mushrooms cool slightly before serving.

Per serving: Calories: 100; Total Fat: 7g; Saturated Fat: 4g; Cholesterol: 21mg; Sodium: 123mg; Carbohydrates: 5g; Fiber: 1g; Protein: 5g

Sweet and Spicy Nuts

These easy-to-make, unassuming nuts are a sleeper hit at parties. The combination of sweet, salty, and spicy sneaks up on you. Your guests will try a few to be polite, then try a couple more, and pretty soon, they'll be jostling to grab the last ones in the bowl. If you can keep any around long enough, they're fabulous in Asian-inspired salads, but they're equally great on a hot fudge sundae. Weird, I know, but true.

DAIRY-FREE, GLUTEN-FREE, VEGETARIAN, UNDER 30 MINUTES, UNDER 5 INGREDIENTS

PREP TIME: 5 minutes
AIR ROAST: 15 minutes
TOTAL TIME: 20 minutes

SUBSTITUTION: These are just as good with pecans—in fact, many people I've given the recipe to prefer them to walnuts.

1 pound walnut halves and pieces

½ cup granulated sugar

1 teaspoon cayenne pepper, or to taste

3 tablespoons vegetable oil or walnut oil

½ teaspoon fine salt, or to taste

1. Place the nuts in a large bowl and cover with boiling water. Let them steep for a minute or two.

2. While the nuts are steeping, mix the sugar and cayenne together in a small bowl (1 teaspoon of cayenne produces nuts that are spicy but not too hot; use more or less to your taste).

3. Drain the nuts and return them to the bowl. Add the sugar mixture and oil. Stir until the sugar melts and the nuts are coated evenly. Spread the nuts in a single layer on the sheet pan.

4. Select AIR ROAST, set temperature to 325°F, and set time to 15 minutes. Select START/PAUSE to begin preheating.

5. Once the unit has preheated, slide the pan into the oven.

CONTINUED ▶

6. After 7 or 8 minutes, remove the pan from the oven. Stir the nuts; they should be browning and fragrant. Return the pan to the oven and continue cooking, but check the nuts frequently. They can go from brown to burned pretty quickly.

7. When cooking is complete, the nuts should be dark golden brown. Remove the pan from the oven. Sprinkle the nuts with the salt and let cool. They can be frozen in an airtight container for up to 1 month.

Per (¼ cup) serving: *Calories: 233; Total Fat: 21g; Saturated Fat: 2g; Cholesterol: 0mg; Sodium: 74mg; Carbohydrates: 10g; Fiber: 2g; Protein: 4g*

Crispy Lemon-Pepper Wings

Over the years, we've tried cooking wings any number of ways—fried, battered, sous vide, pressure cooked, grilled—you name it. It turns out that roasting at high heat is the way to go. A touch of baking powder helps the wings brown and crisp. For the absolute best results, try to let the rubbed wings rest before cooking.

DAIRY-FREE, NUT-FREE, GLUTEN-FREE, UNDER 30 MINUTES, UNDER 5 INGREDIENTS

PREP TIME: 5 minutes
AIR FRY: 24 minutes
TOTAL TIME: 29 minutes

SUBSTITUTION: If you can't find salt-free lemon pepper, skip the salt and use 2 tablespoons of lemon pepper seasoning.

VARIATION: You can use any seasonings you like for the wings; use the previous proportions as a guide. Just make sure the mix doesn't contain any sugar as it will burn during cooking.

2 pounds chicken wing flats and drumettes (about 16 to 20 pieces)

1½ teaspoons kosher salt or ¾ teaspoon fine salt

1½ teaspoons baking powder

4½ teaspoons salt-free lemon pepper seasoning (I use Penzey's Sunny Spain mix)

1. Place the wings in a large bowl.

2. In a small bowl, stir together the salt, baking powder, and seasoning mix. Sprinkle the mixture over the wings and toss thoroughly to coat the wings. (This works best with your hands.) If you have time, let the wings sit for 20 to 30 minutes. Place the wings on the sheet pan, making sure they don't crowd each other too much.

3. Select AIR FRY, set temperature to 375°F, and set time to 24 minutes. Select START/PAUSE to begin preheating.

4. Once preheated, slide the pan into the oven.

5. After 12 minutes, remove the pan from the oven. Using tongs, turn the wings over. Rotate the pan 180 degrees and return the pan to the oven to continue cooking.

6. When cooking is complete, the wings should be dark golden brown and a bit charred in places. Remove the pan from the oven and let cool for before serving.

Per serving: Calories: 294; Total Fat: 20g; Saturated Fat: 5g; Cholesterol: 72mg; Sodium: 381mg; Carbohydrates: 10g; Fiber: 0g; Protein: 18g

Savory Sausage Rolls

SERVES 12

With frozen puff pastry sheets and pre-seasoned breakfast sausage, it's easy to make this British pub favorite at home. I usually make both rolls and freeze one (uncooked) to have on hand for emergency appetizers, like when unexpected guests show up or (much more likely) I need an afternoon pick-me-up. If you slice before freezing, the rolls can go straight from the freezer to oven.

DAIRY-FREE, NUT-FREE, UNDER 30 MINUTES

PREP TIME: 15 minutes
AIR ROAST: 15 minutes
TOTAL TIME: 27 minutes

HACK IT: You can skip the seasonings and just use plain breakfast sausage, or a flavored variety, to save time. Just stir in the egg and bread crumbs and continue with the recipe.

1 pound bulk breakfast sausage

½ cup finely chopped onion (about ½ medium onion)

1 garlic clove, minced or pressed

½ teaspoon dried sage (optional)

¼ teaspoon cayenne pepper

½ teaspoon dried mustard

1 large egg, beaten lightly

½ cup fresh bread crumbs

2 sheets (1 package) frozen puff pastry, thawed

All-purpose flour, for dusting

1. In a medium bowl, break up the sausage. Add the onion, garlic, sage (if using), cayenne, mustard, egg, and bread crumbs. Mix to combine. Divide the sausage mixture in half and tightly wrap each half in plastic wrap. Refrigerate for 5 to 10 minutes.

2. Lay out one of the pastry sheets on a lightly floured cutting board. Using a rolling pin, lightly roll out the pastry to smooth out the dough. Take out one of the sausage packages and form the sausage into a long roll (it's easiest to do this while the sausage is in the plastic wrap). Remove the plastic wrap and place the sausage on top of the puff pastry about 1 inch from one of the long edges. Roll the pastry around the sausage and pinch the edges of the dough together to seal. Repeat with the other pastry sheet and sausage. Slice the logs into lengths about 1½ inches long. (If you have the time, freeze the logs for

10 minutes or so before slicing; it's much easier to slice.) Place the sausage rolls on the sheet pan, cut-side down.

3. Select AIR ROAST, set temperature to 350°F, and set time to 15 minutes. Select START/PAUSE to begin preheating.

4. Once the unit has preheated, slide the pan into the oven.

5. After 7 or 8 minutes, rotate the pan 180 degrees and continue cooking.

6. When cooking is complete, the rolls will be golden brown and sizzling. Remove the pan from the oven and let cool for 5 minutes or so. If you like, serve them with honey mustard for dipping.

Per serving: *Calories: 330; Total Fat: 23g; Saturated Fat: 7g; Cholesterol: 41mg; Sodium: 432mg; Carbohydrates: 21g; Fiber: 1g; Protein: 10g*

Pepperoni Pizza Bites

SERVES 8

I've tried what are called pepperoni rolls, well known in a couple of Eastern states and virtually unheard of elsewhere. They're made with a yeast dough, wrapped around pepperoni and sometimes cheese, and then baked. They're good. They're time consuming. These little pinwheels are much easier, faster, and much more delicious.

NUT-FREE, FAMILY FAVORITE, 5-INGREDIENT, UNDER 30 MINUTES

PREP TIME: 12 minutes
AIR ROAST: 16 minutes
TOTAL TIME: 26 minutes

VARIATION: For a vegetarian version, substitute finely chopped cooked mushrooms for the pepperoni, or just use more cheese. Sprinkle with a few red pepper flakes.

½ cup (2 ounces) pepperoni (very finely chopped)

1 cup finely shredded mozzarella cheese

¼ cup Marinara Sauce (page 195) or store-bought variety

1 (8-ounce) can crescent roll dough

All-purpose flour, for dusting

1. In a small bowl, toss together the pepperoni and cheese. Stir in the marinara sauce. (If you have one, this is a good time to use a food processor. Then you don't have to chop everything so fine; just dump everything in and pulse a few times to mix.)

2. Unroll the dough onto a lightly floured cutting board. Separate it into 4 rectangles. Firmly pinch the perforations together and pat or roll the dough pieces flat.

3. Divide the cheese mixture evenly between the rectangles and spread it out over the dough, leaving a ¼-inch border. Roll a rectangle up tightly, starting with the short end. Pinch the edge down to seal the roll. Repeat with the remaining rolls. If you have time, refrigerate or freeze the rolls for 5 to 10 minutes to firm up. This makes slicing easier.

4. Slice the rolls into 4 or 5 even slices. Place the slices on the sheet pan, leaving a few inches between each.

5. Select AIR ROAST, set temperature to 350ºF, and set time to 12 minutes. Select START/PAUSE to begin preheating.

6. Once the unit has preheated, slide the pan into the oven.

7. After 6 minutes, rotate the pan 180 degrees and continue cooking.

8. When cooking is complete, the rolls will be golden brown with crisp edges. Remove the pan from the oven. If you like, serve with additional marinara sauce for dipping.

Per serving: *Calories: 179; Total Fat: 11g; Saturated Fat: 5g; Cholesterol: 19mg; Sodium: 456mg; Carbohydrates: 12g; Fiber: 0g; Protein: 7g*

Mini Tuna Melts with Scallions and Capers

When I was growing up, tuna melts were one of my favorite sandwiches. When I got my first apartment and before I learned how to cook much, I made them frequently. I like my sandwiches crisp on the bottom, so I coat the bread with butter. I use oil-packed tuna because I prefer the flavor, but feel free to use water-packed if that's what you like. Feel free to use your own tuna salad recipe here; just make sure it's not too wet, so it doesn't soak through the bread.

NUT-FREE, FAMILY FAVORITE, UNDER 30 MINUTES

PREP TIME: 12 minutes
AIR ROAST: 6 minutes
TOTAL TIME: 18 minutes

SUBSTITUTION: I always have a jar of capers on hand, but if you're not as weird as I am, you can substitute chopped dill pickles, or just make a caper-free, pickle-free tuna salad.

2 (5- to 6-ounce) cans oil-packed tuna, drained

1 small stalk celery, chopped

1 large scallion, chopped

⅓ cup mayonnaise, or more to taste

1 tablespoon capers, drained

¼ teaspoon celery salt (optional)

1 tablespoon chopped fresh dill (optional)

12 slices cocktail rye bread

2 tablespoons butter, melted

6 slices sharp cheddar or Swiss-style cheese (about 3 ounces)

1. In a medium bowl, mix together the tuna, celery, scallion, mayonnaise, capers, celery salt, and dill (if using).

2. Brush one side of the bread slices with the butter. Arrange the bread slices on the pan, buttered-sides down. Scoop a heaping tablespoon of the tuna mixture on each slice of bread, spreading it out evenly to the edges.

3. Cut the cheese slices to fit the dimensions of the bread and place a cheese slice on each piece.

4. Select AIR ROAST, set temperature to 375ºF, and set time to 6 minutes. Select START/PAUSE to begin preheating.

5. Once the unit has preheated, slide the pan into the oven.

6. After 4 minutes, remove the pan from the oven and check the tuna melts. They usually take at least 5 minutes, but depending on the cheese you're using and the temperature of the tuna salad, it can take anywhere from 4 to 6 minutes. The tuna melts are done when the cheese has melted and the tuna is heated through. If needed, continue cooking.

7. When cooking is complete, remove the pan from the oven. Use a spatula to transfer the tuna melts to a cutting board and slice each one in half diagonally (this will make them easier to eat). Serve warm.

Per serving: Calories: 256; Total Fat: 16g; Saturated Fat: 5g; Cholesterol: 27mg; Sodium: 437mg; Carbohydrates: 14g; Fiber: 2g; Protein: 13g

Prosciutto-Wrapped Party Pears

SERVES 8

I first tried this appetizer at a Christmas party years ago, and soon after it went into my party rotation. A little sweet, a little salty, with a touch of acid from the balsamic—it covers all the taste bases. You can prepare the pears a couple of hours ahead of time and just pop them into the oven when you're ready to cook them. And the recipe is a cinch to double if your party is large.

NUT-FREE, DAIRY-FREE, GLUTEN-FREE, 5-INGREDIENT, UNDER 30 MINUTES

PREP TIME: 12 minutes
AIR BROIL: 6 minutes
TOTAL TIME: 18 minutes

SUBSTITUTION: If you don't have aged balsamic and don't want to invest in a bottle, you can use a less expensive version. Instead of drizzling on the finished pears, baste the pears with a thin coat when you turn them over.

2 large ripe Anjou pears

4 thin slices Parma prosciutto (about 2 ounces)

2 teaspoons aged balsamic vinegar

1. Peel the pears. Slice into 6 or 8 wedges (depending on the size of the pears) and cut out the core from each wedge.

2. Cut the prosciutto into long strips (one strip per pear wedge). Wrap each pear wedge with a strip of prosciutto. Place the wrapped pears on the sheet pan.

3. Select AIR BROIL, set temperature HIGH, and set time to 6 minutes. Select START/PAUSE to begin preheating.

4. Once the unit has preheated, slide the pan into the oven.

5. After 2 or 3 minutes, check the pears. The pears should be turned over if the prosciutto is beginning to crisp up and brown. Return the pan to the oven and continue cooking.

6. When cooking is complete, remove the pan from the oven. Serve the pears warm or at room temperature with a drizzle of the balsamic vinegar.

Per serving: Calories: 47; Total Fat: 1g; Saturated Fat: 1g; Cholesterol: 6mg; Sodium: 136mg; Carbohydrates: 8g; Fiber: 2g; Protein: 2g

Garlic-Parmesan Crunchy Snack Mix

MAKES ABOUT 6 CUPS

I have to admit that I'm not a big fan of regular Chex mix. But I do like this variation, which is based on a snack my Dad used to make with oyster crackers, butter, and Parmesan cheese. I still like it with just the crackers, but the cereal and sesame sticks add different textures and flavors. If you ever get tired of eating it out of hand, it makes a wonderful substitute for croutons on tossed green salad.

NUT-FREE, VEGETARIAN, UNDER 30 MINUTES

PREP TIME: 10 minutes
AIR ROAST: 6 minutes
TOTAL TIME: 16 minutes

VARIATION: Instead of granulated garlic, use your favorite spice mixture. (I like Old Bay or Cajun spice blend.) Omit the salt if your spice mixture contains it.

2 cups oyster crackers

2 cups Chex-style cereal (rice, corn, or wheat, or a combination)

1 cup sesame sticks

8 tablespoons unsalted butter, melted

⅔ cup finely grated Parmesan cheese

1½ teaspoon granulated garlic

½ teaspoon kosher salt or ¼ teaspoon fine salt

1. Place the oyster crackers in a large bowl. Add the cereal and sesame sticks. Drizzle with the butter and sprinkle on the cheese, garlic, and salt. Toss to coat. Place the mix on the sheet pan in an even layer.

2. Select AIR ROAST, set temperature to 350ºF, and set time to 6 minutes. Select START/PAUSE to begin preheating.

3. Once the unit has preheated, slide the pan into the oven.

4. About halfway through cooking, remove the pan and stir the mixture. Return the pan to the oven and continue cooking.

5. When cooking is complete, the mix should be lightly browned and fragrant. Let cool. The mixture can be stored at room temperature in an airtight container for 3 to 4 days.

Per (⅓ cup) serving: Calories: 83; Total Fat: 7g; Saturated Fat: 4g; Cholesterol: 16mg; Sodium: 148mg; Carbohydrates: 4g; Fiber: 0g; Protein: 2g

Chiles Rellenos–Style Nachos

SERVES 6

Many people assume that more is better when it comes to nachos, but I find the key is restraint. Pick a good melty cheese and one or two additions, and stop. These nachos are reminiscent of chiles rellenos, but way easier to make.

NUT-FREE, GLUTEN-FREE, VEGETARIAN, UNDER 30 MINUTES

PREP TIME: 10 minutes
AIR ROAST: 10 minutes
TOTAL TIME: 20 minutes

HACK IT: I like the tomato sauce, which I've modeled after the sauce I make for chiles rellenos, but if you prefer, just use your favorite mild tomato-based salsa instead.

8 ounces tortilla chips

3 cups shredded Monterey Jack cheese

2 (7-ounce) cans chopped green chiles, drained

1 (8-ounce) can tomato sauce

¼ teaspoon granulated garlic

¼ teaspoon dried oregano

¼ teaspoon freshly ground black pepper

Pinch cinnamon

Pinch cayenne pepper

1. Arrange the tortilla chips close together in a single layer on the sheet pan. Sprinkle half of the cheese over the chips. Arrange the green chiles over the cheese as evenly as possible, then cover with the remaining cheese.

2. Select AIR ROAST, set temperature to 375°F, and set time to 10 minutes. Select START/PAUSE to begin preheating.

3. Once the unit has preheated, slide the pan into the oven.

4. After 5 minutes, rotate the pan 180 degrees and continue cooking.

5. While the nachos are cooking, stir together the tomato sauce, garlic, oregano, pepper, cinnamon, and cayenne in a small bowl.

6. When cooking is complete, the cheese will be melted and starting to crisp around the edges of the pan. Remove the pan from the oven. Drizzle a couple of tablespoons of the sauce over the nachos and serve the rest of the sauce for dipping (you can warm it up, if you like).

Per serving: Calories: 428; Total Fat: 26g; Saturated Fat: 12g; Cholesterol: 50mg; Sodium: 825mg; Carbohydrates: 32g; Fiber: 3g; Protein: 17g

Classic Pizza Margherita, *page 70*

5

Vegetarian Mains

Three-Cheese Zucchini and Spinach Rolls

SERVES 6

These rolls can take some time to perfect, so I like to break them out when I really want to impress friends. It takes some practice to get the zucchini cut into thin, even slices (or try out your mandoline skills), but once you get it right, the rest of the recipe goes pretty quickly. The time is worth it, in my opinion; it's an impressive dish that always delights.

NUT-FREE, GLUTEN-FREE, VEGETARIAN

PREP TIME: 15 minutes
AIR ROAST: 18 minutes
TOTAL TIME: 33 minutes

DID YOU KNOW:
Zucchini, like most squashes, contain a lot of water. Salting the slices before rolling them removes some of that liquid, so that the cooked dish isn't a watery mess. Plus, the salting process softens up the flesh, so the slices will be malleable enough to roll without breaking. Rinsing and then blotting the slices dry removes excess salt, so the slices are seasoned perfectly.

- 3 large zucchini
- 2½ teaspoons kosher salt or 1¼ teaspoons fine salt, divided
- 1½ cups cooked chopped spinach
- 1½ cups whole milk ricotta cheese
- ½ cup freshly grated Parmesan cheese
- 1½ cups shredded mozzarella, divided
- 1 large egg, lightly beaten
- 1 teaspoon Italian seasoning or ½ teaspoon each dried basil and oregano
- Freshly ground black pepper
- Cooking oil spray
- 1½ cups Marinara Sauce (page 195) or store-bought variety

1. Cut off the ends of the zucchini and peel several strips off one side to make a flat base. Use a large Y-shaped peeler or sharp cheese plane to cut long slices about ⅛-inch thick. When you get to a point where you can't get any more slices, set that zucchini aside and start on the next. You need 8 good slices per squash, for a total of 24 slices (a few extra never hurts). Save the rest of the zucchini pieces for another recipe, such as the Ratatouille Casserole (page 80).

2. Salt one side of the zucchini slices with 1 teaspoon of kosher salt. Place the slices salted-side down on a rack placed over a baking sheet. Salt the other sides with another teaspoon of kosher salt. Let the slices sit for 10 minutes, or until they start to exude water (you'll see it

beading up on the surface of the slices and dripping onto the baking sheet).

3. While the zucchini sits, in a medium bowl, combine the spinach, ricotta, Parmesan cheese, ¾ cup of mozzarella, egg, Italian seasoning, remaining ½ teaspoon of kosher salt, and pepper.

4. Spray the sheet pan with cooking oil spray.

5. Rinse the zucchini slices off and blot them dry with a paper towel. Spread about 2 tablespoons of the ricotta mixture evenly along each zucchini slice. Roll up the slice and place each seam-side down on the prepared sheet pan. Place the rolls so they touch, working from the center of the pan out toward the edges. Repeat with remaining zucchini slices and filling. Top the rolls with the marinara sauce and sprinkle with the remaining ¾ cup of mozzarella.

6. Select AIR ROAST, set temperature to 375°F, and set time to 18 minutes. Select START/PAUSE to begin preheating.

7. Once the unit has preheated, slide the pan into the oven.

8. After about 15 minutes, check the rolls. They are done when the cheese is melted and beginning to brown, and the filling is bubbling. If necessary, continue cooking for another 3 to 4 minutes.

9. When cooking is complete, remove the pan from the oven. Serve.

Per serving: *Calories: 235; Total Fat: 14g; Saturated Fat: 8g; Cholesterol: 76mg; Sodium: 622mg; Carbohydrates: 12g; Fiber: 4g; Protein: 18g*

Classic Pizza Margherita

SERVES 4

Sometimes with pizza, simpler is better. That's why pizza Margherita, with nothing but cheese, tomatoes, and basil, has always been one of my favorites. In my version, the tomatoes and basil go on after baking for a delightful mix of flavors and textures. Crisp crust, melty cheese, tangy cool tomatoes, and the herbal note of fresh basil—it's hard to imagine a better combination.

NUT-FREE, VEGETARIAN,
FAMILY FAVORITE,
UNDER 30 MINUTES

PREP TIME: 15 minutes
AIR ROAST: 12 minutes
TOTAL TIME: 30 minutes

VARIATION: If you ever get tired of this pizza (which you won't), feel free to replace the tomatoes and basil with other vegetables. Cooked mushrooms are delicious (add them with the Parmesan cheese), as are marinated artichokes (add after cooking).

1 pound store-bought pizza dough

2 tablespoons extra-virgin olive oil, divided

½ cup Marinara Sauce (page 195) or store-bought variety

6 ounces shredded mozzarella cheese

½ cup coarsely shredded Parmesan cheese (about 1½ ounces)

2 large tomatoes, seeded and chopped (about 1½ cups)

¼ teaspoon kosher salt or ⅛ teaspoon fine salt

¼ cup chopped fresh basil

2 teaspoons wine vinegar

1. Punch down the pizza dough to release as much air as possible. Place the dough on the sheet pan and press it out toward the edges. The dough will likely spring back and shrink. Be patient and keep working at it, leaving it alone to relax for a few minutes from time to time. As it stretches, I find it helpful to coat my fingers with 1 tablespoon of olive oil and then poke the dough lightly with my fingertips to keep it from shrinking as much. Don't worry if you can't get it all the way to the pan's edges.

2. Spread the marinara sauce over the dough. You'll be able to see the dough through the sauce in places; you don't want a thick coating. Evenly top the sauce with the mozzarella cheese.

3. Select AIR ROAST, set temperature to 425ºF, and set time to 12 minutes. Select START/PAUSE to begin preheating.

4. Once the unit has preheated, slide the pan into the oven.

5. After about 8 minutes, remove the pan from the oven. Sprinkle the Parmesan cheese over the pizza. Return the pan to the oven. Alternatively, if you like a crisp crust, use a pizza peel or cake lifter (or even a very large spatula) to slide the pizza off the pan and directly onto the oven rack. Continue cooking.

6. While the pizza cooks, place the tomatoes in a colander or fine-mesh strainer and sprinkle with the salt. Let them drain for a few minutes, then place in a small bowl. Mix in the remaining 1 tablespoon of olive oil, basil, and vinegar.

7. When cooking is complete, the cheese on top will be lightly browned and bubbling and the crust a deep golden brown. Remove the pizza from the sheet pan, if you haven't already, and place it on a wire rack to cool for a few minutes (a rack will keep the crust from getting soggy as it cools). Distribute the tomato mixture evenly over the pizza, then transfer to a cutting board to slice and serve.

Per serving: *Calories: 512; Total Fat: 25g; Saturated Fat: 9g; Cholesterol: 45mg; Sodium: 764mg; Carbohydrates: 65g; Fiber: 6g; Protein: 24g*

Cheese and Mushroom Enchiladas with Spicy Beans and Corn

SERVES 4

Since I began making my own enchiladas, I've become an admitted enchilada snob. I used to think enchiladas were all about lots of spicy tomato sauce and tons of cheese over meat-stuffed tortillas. And honestly, there's nothing wrong with those—what's not to like? But enchiladas are really about tortillas and chiles, and traditionally, they don't go in a casserole dish with tons of sauce and cheese. My version kind of takes the middle road. I do coat my tortillas liberally with a chile-based sauce, with minimal fillings. But I also top them with cheese, and I do bake them.

NUT-FREE, GLUTEN-FREE, VEGETARIAN, UNDER 30 MINUTES

PREP TIME: 10 minutes
BAKE: 17 minutes
TOTAL TIME: 27 minutes

8 (6-inch) corn tortillas

Cooking oil spray or vegetable oil, for brushing

1 (15-ounce) can black beans, drained

¾ cups frozen corn, thawed

1 teaspoon chili powder

2 tablespoons salsa (I like Frontera brand salsas)

1½ cups Red Enchilada Sauce (page 198) or store-bought variety (Rosarita is a good brand)

1 recipe Oven-Roasted Mushrooms (page 201)

8 ounces shredded Monterey Jack cheese

1. Spray the tortillas on both sides with cooking oil spray or brush lightly with the oil. Arrange them on the sheet pan, overlapping as little as possible.

2. Select AIR ROAST, set temperature to 325ºF, and set time to 5 minutes. Select START/PAUSE to begin preheating.

3. Once the unit has preheated, slide the pan into the oven.

4. While the tortillas warm, place the beans in a medium bowl. Add the corn, chili powder, and salsa and stir to combine. Transfer the mixture to a large sheet of aluminum foil. Fold the foil over the mixture and seal the edges to create a packet. Set aside.

5. After 5 minutes, remove the pan from the oven. Stack the tortillas on a plate and cover with foil.

6. Pour about half of the enchilada sauce on one end of the sheet pan. Place a tortilla in the sauce, turning it over to coat it thoroughly. Spoon a couple of tablespoons of mushrooms down the middle of the tortilla and top with a couple tablespoons of cheese. Roll up the tortilla and place it seam-side down on one edge of the pan. Repeat with the remaining tortillas, adding more sauce to the pan as necessary, forming a row of enchiladas from one side of the pan to the other. (Leave room along one side for the beans.) You may not use all the mushrooms, and you should have about ⅓ cup of cheese remaining.

7. Spoon most of the remaining sauce over the enchiladas. You don't want them drowning, but they should be nicely coated. Sprinkle the remaining cheese over the enchiladas.

8. Place the packet of beans and corn next to the row of enchiladas.

9. Select AIR ROAST, set temperature to 350°F, and set time to 12 minutes. Select START/PAUSE to begin preheating.

10. Once the unit has preheated, slide the pan into the oven.

11. When cooking is complete, the cheese will be melted and the sauce will be bubbling. Remove the pan from the oven. Open the beans and corn and stir gently. Adjust the seasoning, adding salt or more salsa as desired.

Per serving: *Calories: 446; Total Fat: 20g; Saturated Fat: 11g; Cholesterol: 50mg; Sodium: 548mg; Carbohydrates: 46g; Fiber: 11g; Protein: 25g*

Eggs with Roasted Asparagus and Tomatoes

SERVES 4

The mix of roasted asparagus and tomatoes with soft-cooked eggs makes this a lovely brunch dish or light lunch. For a more substantial dish, double up on the eggs and serve with a crusty baguette.

DAIRY-FREE,
NUT-FREE, GLUTEN-
FREE, VEGETARIAN,
5-INGREDIENT, UNDER
30 MINUTES

PREP TIME: 10 minutes
AIR ROAST: 12 minutes
TOTAL TIME: 27 minutes

2 pounds asparagus, trimmed

3 tablespoons extra-virgin olive oil, divided

1 teaspoon kosher salt or ½ teaspoon fine salt, divided

1 pint cherry tomatoes

4 large eggs

¼ teaspoon freshly ground black pepper

1. Place the asparagus on the sheet pan. Drizzle with 2 tablespoons of olive oil and use tongs (or your hands) to toss the asparagus to coat it with the oil. Sprinkle with ½ teaspoon of kosher salt.

2. Select AIR ROAST, set temperature to 375°F, and set time to 12 minutes. Select START/PAUSE to begin preheating.

3. Once the oven has preheated, slide the pan into the oven.

4. While the asparagus is cooking, place the tomatoes in a medium bowl and drizzle with the remaining 1 tablespoon of olive oil. Toss to coat.

5. After 6 minutes, remove the pan from the oven. Using tongs, toss the asparagus; it should be starting to get crisp at the tips. Spread the asparagus evenly in the center of the pan. Add the tomatoes around the perimeter of the pan. Return the pan to the oven and continue cooking.

6. After 2 minutes, remove the pan from the oven.

CONTINUED ▶

7. Carefully crack the eggs over the asparagus, being careful to space them out so they aren't touching. Sprinkle the eggs with the remaining ½ teaspoon of kosher salt and the pepper. Return the pan to the oven and continue cooking. Cook for another 3 to 7 minutes, depending on how you like your eggs.

8. When cooking is complete, use a large spatula to transfer an egg with the asparagus underneath to plates. Spoon the tomatoes onto the plates.

Per serving: *Calories: 223; Total Fat: 16g; Saturated Fat: 3g; Cholesterol: 186mg; Sodium: 660mg; Carbohydrates: 13g; Fiber: 6g; Protein: 12g*

Stuffed Rainbow Peppers

These unusual stuffed peppers are reminiscent of Middle Eastern cuisine with chickpeas, lots of garlic, olive oil, parsley, and cumin. They're really pretty with a mix of bell peppers, but any colors will be delicious.

DAIRY-FREE, NUT-FREE, VEGETARIAN, VEGAN, UNDER 30 MINUTES

PREP TIME: 10 minutes
AIR ROAST: 18 minutes
TOTAL TIME: 28 minutes

VARIATION: Trade the Middle Eastern flavors for Mexican by replacing the chickpeas with black or pinto beans, replacing the parsley with cilantro, and the roasted red peppers with canned diced green chiles. Top with Monterey Jack cheese instead of panko.

- 4 medium red, green, or yellow bell peppers
- 4 tablespoons extra-virgin olive oil, divided
- ½ teaspoon kosher salt or ¼ teaspoon fine salt, divided
- 1 (15-ounce) can chickpeas
- 3 garlic cloves, minced or pressed
- ½ small onion, finely chopped (about ½ cup)
- 1½ cups Oven Rice (page 203) or cooked white rice
- ½ cup diced roasted red peppers
- ¼ cup chopped parsley
- ¼ teaspoon freshly ground black pepper
- ½ teaspoon cumin
- ¾ cup panko bread crumbs

1. Cut the peppers in half through the stem and remove the seeds and ribs. You can either leave the stem attached or cut it out, as you like. Brush the peppers inside and out with 1 tablespoon of olive oil. Sprinkle the insides with ¼ teaspoon of kosher salt. Place the peppers cut-side up on the sheet pan.

2. Pour the beans with their liquid into a large bowl. Using a potato masher, lightly mash the beans. Add the remaining ¼ teaspoon of kosher salt, 1 tablespoon of olive oil, the garlic, onion, rice, roasted red peppers, parsley, black pepper, and cumin. Stir to combine. Spoon the mixture into the bell pepper halves.

3. In a small bowl, stir together the panko and remaining 2 tablespoons of olive oil. Top the peppers with the panko mixture.

CONTINUED ▶

4. Select AIR ROAST, set temperature to 375ºF, and set time to 18 minutes. Select START/PAUSE to begin preheating.

5. Once the unit has preheated, slide the pan into the oven.

6. After about 12 minutes, remove the pan from the oven. If the panko is browning unevenly, rotate the pan 180 degrees. Return the pan to the oven and continue cooking.

7. When cooking is complete, the peppers should be slightly wrinkled, and the panko should be deep golden brown.

Per serving: *Calories: 405; Total Fat: 17g; Saturated Fat: 2g; Cholesterol: 0mg; Sodium: 167mg; Carbohydrates: 56g; Fiber: 8g; Protein: 11g*

Ratatouille Casserole

When I first started cooking for myself, I invested in Julia Child's Mastering the Art of French Cooking. *At the time, I had a good deal of free time, so I made many recipes, some of which are still among my favorites. She had a recipe for ratatouille, a stewed vegetable dish, which called for cooking all of the vegetables separately. It seemed extreme, but I faithfully followed the directions. It was good, but not worth the trouble. So now I combine everything and cook it together, and I'm very happy.*

DAIRY-FREE, NUT-FREE, VEGETARIAN, VEGAN OPTION, UNDER 30 MINUTES

PREP TIME: 10 minutes
AIR ROAST: 12 minutes
TOTAL TIME: 27 minutes

VARIATION: Instead of topping the ratatouille with bread crumbs, serve it over polenta. Add slices of Oven Polenta (page 204) to the pan at the beginning of cooking, and top the finished dish with Parmesan cheese.

- 1 small eggplant, peeled and sliced ½-inch thick
- 1 medium zucchini, sliced ½-inch thick
- 2 teaspoons kosher salt or 1 teaspoon fine salt, divided
- 4 tablespoons extra-virgin olive oil, divided
- 1 small onion, chopped (about 1 cup)
- 3 garlic cloves, minced or pressed
- 1 small green bell pepper, cut into ½-inch chunks (about 1 cup)
- 1 small red bell pepper, cut into ½-inch chunks (about 1 cup)
- ½ teaspoon dried oregano
- ¼ teaspoon freshly ground black pepper
- 1 pint cherry tomatoes
- 2 tablespoons minced fresh basil
- 1 cup panko bread crumbs
- ½ cup grated Parmesan cheese (optional)

1. Salt one side of the eggplant and zucchini slices with ¾ teaspoon of salt. Place the slices salted-side down on a rack placed over a baking sheet. Salt the other sides with another ¾ teaspoon of salt. Let the slices sit for 10 minutes, or until they start to exude water (it will bead up on the surface of the slices and drip down into the baking sheet). Rinse the slices off and blot them dry with a paper towel. Cut the zucchini slices into quarters and the eggplant slices into eighths.

2. Place the zucchini and eggplant in a large bowl and add 2 tablespoons of olive oil, the onion, garlic, bell peppers, oregano, and black pepper. Toss to coat the vegetables with the oil. Place the vegetables on the sheet pan.

3. Select AIR ROAST, set temperature to 375°F, and set time to 12 minutes. Select START/PAUSE to begin preheating.

4. Once the unit has preheated, slide the pan into the oven.

5. While the vegetables are cooking, place the tomatoes and basil into the bowl. Add 1 tablespoon of olive oil and the remaining ½ teaspoon of salt.

6. In a small bowl, mix the panko, remaining 1 tablespoon of olive oil, and Parmesan cheese (if using).

7. After 6 minutes, remove the pan from the oven. Add the tomato mixture to the vegetables on the sheet pan and stir to combine. Top with the panko mixture. Return the pan to the oven and continue cooking.

8. When cooking is complete, the vegetables should be tender and the topping golden brown. Remove the pan from the oven and serve.

Per serving: *Calories: 171; Total Fat: 10g; Saturated Fat: 2g; Cholesterol: 0mg; Sodium: 180mg; Carbohydrates: 19g; Fiber: 6g; Protein: 4g*

Kung Pao Tofu

SERVES 4

Tofu, with its subtle flavor, is great paired with a spicy sauce like this one. Crisp vegetables and crunchy peanuts add texture in this quick, easy, and delicious vegan main dish.

DAIRY-FREE,
VEGETARIAN, VEGAN,
UNDER 30 MINUTES

PREP TIME: 10 minutes
AIR ROAST: 10 minutes
TOTAL TIME: 20 minutes

⅓ cup Asian-Style Sauce (page 197)

½ teaspoon red pepper flakes, or more to taste

1 teaspoon cornstarch

1 pound firm or extra-firm tofu, cut into 1-inch cubes

1 small green bell pepper, cut into bite-size pieces

1 small carrot, peeled and cut into ¼-inch-thick coins

3 scallions, sliced, whites and green parts separated

3 tablespoons roasted unsalted peanuts

1. Place the sauce into a large bowl. Add the red pepper flakes and cornstarch, and whisk to combine. Add the tofu, pepper, carrot, and the white parts of the scallions. Toss to coat. Place on the sheet pan in an even layer.

2. Select AIR ROAST, set temperature to 375°F, and set time to 10 minutes. Select START/PAUSE to begin preheating.

3. Once the unit has preheated, slide the pan into the oven.

4. After 6 minutes, remove the pan from the oven. Stir the ingredients. Return the pan to the oven and continue cooking.

5. When cooking is complete, the vegetables should be tender and the sauce thickened. Remove the pan from the oven. Stir in the peanuts and the scallion greens, and serve immediately, plain or over steamed rice.

Per serving: Calories: 177; Total Fat: 10g; Saturated Fat: 1g; Cholesterol: 0mg; Sodium: 222mg; Carbohydrates: 10g; Fiber: 2g; Protein: 14g

Crispy Bean and Cheese Tacos

What's better than tacos? These genius tacos! With this recipe, there's no need to cook the filling and the taco shell separately. Just fill and bake. You'll have spicy, crunchy tacos in no time.

NUT-FREE, VEGETARIAN, UNDER 30 MINUTES

PREP TIME: 12 minutes
AIR FRY: 7 minutes
TOTAL TIME: 19 minutes

VARIATION: If you prefer your tacos with corn tortillas (also gluten-free), you can oil and heat them as in the Cheese and Mushroom Enchiladas (page 72), then proceed to fill and cook them. If you try to fold corn tortillas without that step, they'll crack, and your tacos will leak, and everyone will be sad.

1 (15-ounce) can black beans, drained and rinsed

½ cup prepared salsa (I use Frontera brand Double Roasted Salsa)

1½ teaspoons chili powder

2 tablespoons minced onion

4 ounces grated Monterey Jack cheese (plain or with jalapeños)

8 (6-inch) flour tortillas

2 tablespoons vegetable or extra-virgin olive oil

Shredded lettuce, for serving

1. Place the beans in a medium bowl, preferably one with a flat bottom. Add the salsa and chili powder. Using a potato masher, coarsely mash the beans and salsa. Add the onion and cheese and stir to combine.

2. Lay out the tortillas on a cutting board and divide the filling among them (2 to 3 tablespoons per tortilla). Fold the tortillas over, pressing lightly to even out the filling. Brush the tacos on one side with half the oil, then place them oiled-side down on the sheet pan. Brush the top side with the remaining oil.

3. Select AIR FRY, set temperature to 400°F, and set time to 7 minutes. Select START/PAUSE to begin preheating.

4. Once the unit has preheated, slide the pan into the oven.

5. After 4 minutes, remove the pan from the oven. Turn the tacos over. Return the pan to the oven and continue cooking.

CONTINUED ▶

Crispy Bean and Cheese Tacos continued

6. When cooking is complete, the tacos should be deep golden brown on both sides. Remove the pan from the oven and let cool for a few minutes (the filling will be very hot). Place the tacos on plates and serve with the shredded lettuce, and additional salsa and cheese if desired.

Per serving: *Calories: 567; Total Fat: 25g; Saturated Fat: 8g; Cholesterol: 25mg; Sodium: 1038mg; Carbohydrates: 67g; Fiber: 7g; Protein: 19g*

Spicy Thai Vegetables

SERVES 4

This recipe falls somewhere between a stir-fry and a salad. Roasted vegetables are mixed with raw cabbage and mango slices, and then the whole thing is dressed in a wonderful spicy and tangy dressing. It's a great summertime dinner when you want something light but satisfying.

DAIRY-FREE,
VEGETARIAN, VEGAN,
UNDER 30 MINUTES

PREP TIME: 10 minutes
AIR ROAST: 8 minutes
TOTAL TIME: 20 minutes

SUBSTITUTION: Thai curry pastes sometimes contain fish sauce or shrimp paste, so they may not be vegetarian. If you can't find a vegetarian version, increase the soy sauce and lime juice to 3 tablespoons each, and add a couple of teaspoons of sriracha.

1 small head Napa cabbage, shredded, divided

8 ounces snow peas

1 medium carrot, cut into thin coins

1 red or green bell pepper, sliced into thin strips

1 tablespoon vegetable oil

1 tablespoon sesame oil

2 tablespoons soy sauce

2 tablespoons freshly squeezed lime juice

2 tablespoons brown sugar

2 teaspoons red or green Thai curry paste

1 cup frozen mango slices, thawed

1 serrano chile, seeded and minced

½ cup chopped roasted peanuts or cashews

1. Place half the Napa cabbage in a large bowl. Add the snow peas, carrot, and bell pepper. Drizzle with the vegetable oil and toss to coat. Place on the sheet pan in an even layer.

2. Select AIR ROAST, set temperature to 375ºF, and set time to 8 minutes. Select START/PAUSE to begin preheating.

3. Once the unit has preheated, slide the pan into the oven.

4. While the vegetables cook, in a small bowl, whisk together the sesame oil, soy sauce, lime juice, brown sugar, and curry paste.

CONTINUED ▶

5. When cooking is complete, the vegetables should be crisp-tender. If necessary, continue cooking for a minute or two longer. Remove the pan from the oven and place the vegetables back in the bowl. Add the mango slices, chile, and the remaining Napa cabbage. Add the dressing and toss to coat.

6. Serve topped with the nuts.

Per serving: Calories: 293; Total Fat: 15g; Saturated Fat: 2g; Cholesterol: 0mg; Sodium: 501mg; Carbohydrates: 36g; Fiber: 8g; Protein: 8g

Roasted Portobellos with Peppers and Fontina

SERVES 4

A few years back, my partner Dave and I were teaching a team-building cooking class. The group wanted our "Steakhouse Classics" menu, but they also had some vegetarians in the mix. We came up with this entrée to take the place of the steaks—and all the meat eaters wanted to try it, too.

NUT-FREE, GLUTEN-FREE, VEGETARIAN, UNDER 30 MINUTES

PREP TIME: 15 minutes
AIR ROAST: 12 minutes
AIR BROIL: 3 minutes
TOTAL TIME: 30 minutes

VARIATION: Fill the mushrooms with the stuffing mixture from the Stuffed Rainbow Peppers (page 77).

- 8 portobello mushroom caps, each about 3 inches across
- 4 tablespoons sherry vinegar or white wine vinegar
- 1 tablespoon fresh thyme leaves or 1 teaspoon dried
- 6 garlic cloves, minced or pressed, divided
- 1 teaspoon Dijon mustard
- 1 teaspoon kosher salt or ½ teaspoon fine salt, divided
- ¼ cup plus 3¼ teaspoons extra-virgin olive oil, divided
- 1 small green bell pepper, thinly sliced
- 1 small red or yellow bell pepper, thinly sliced
- 1 small onion, thinly sliced
- ¼ teaspoon red pepper flakes
- Several grinds freshly ground black pepper
- 4 ounces shredded Fontina cheese or other mild melting cheese

1. Rinse off any dirt from the mushroom caps and pat dry.

2. In a small bowl, whisk together the vinegar, thyme, 4 minced garlic cloves, mustard, and ½ teaspoon of kosher salt. Slowly pour in ¼ cup of olive oil, whisking constantly, until an emulsion forms. Alternatively, place the ingredients in a small jar with a tight-fitting lid and shake. Measure out 2 tablespoons and set aside.

3. Place the mushrooms in a resealable plastic bag and add the marinade. Seal the bag, squeezing out as much air as possible. Massage the mushrooms to coat them in the marinade. If you have the time, let marinate about

CONTINUED ▶

20 minutes at room temperature, turning the bag over after 10 minutes.

4. In a medium bowl, place the bell peppers, onion, remaining 2 minced garlic cloves, red pepper flakes, remaining ½ teaspoon of salt, and black pepper. Drizzle the remaining 3¼ teaspoons of olive oil over the vegetables and toss to coat.

5. Remove the mushrooms from the marinade and place them gill-side down on one end of the sheet pan. Place the bell pepper mixture on the other side of the pan.

6. Select AIR ROAST, set temperature to 375ºF, and set time to 12 minutes. Select START/PAUSE to begin preheating.

7. Once preheated, slide the pan into the oven.

8. After 7 minutes, remove the pan from the oven. Stir the peppers and turn the mushrooms over. Return the pan to the oven and continue cooking.

9. When cooking is complete, the peppers are tender and browned in places, and the mushrooms have shrunk somewhat. Remove the pan from the oven. Transfer the pepper mixture to a cutting board and coarsely chop.

10. Brush the mushrooms on both sides with the reserved 2 tablespoons marinade. Fill the caps with the pepper mixture. Sprinkle the cheese over the stuffing.

11. Select BROIL, set temperature to HIGH, and set time to 3 minutes. Select START/PAUSE to begin preheating.

12. Once preheated, slide the pan into the oven. The mushrooms are done when the cheese is melted and bubbling. Remove the pan and garnish with fresh thyme or parsley, if desired.

Per serving: Calories: 342; Total Fat: 27g; Saturated Fat: 8g; Cholesterol: 33mg; Sodium: 306mg; Carbohydrates: 17g; Fiber: 4g; Protein: 13g

Tortellini Primavera

SERVES 4

Pasta Primavera is now a classic in Italian American restaurants. It's typically made with long pasta, like spaghetti or fettuccini, but who says you can't substitute cheese tortellini? Not me. If you start with frozen tortellini, the pasta and vegetables are cooked at about the same time, and the sauce kind of makes itself. Not bad for a quick weekday dinner!

NUT-FREE, VEGETARIAN, UNDER 30 MINUTES

PREP TIME: 10 minutes
BAKE: 11 minutes
AIR ROAST: 5 minutes
TOTAL TIME: 26 minutes

- ½ pound asparagus, trimmed and cut into 1-inch pieces
- 8 ounces sugar snap peas, trimmed
- 1 tablespoon extra-virgin olive oil
- 2 teaspoons kosher salt or 1 teaspoon fine salt, divided
- 1½ cups water
- 1 (20-ounce) package frozen cheese tortellini
- 1 cup heavy (whipping) cream
- 2 garlic cloves, minced
- 1 cup cherry tomatoes, halved
- ½ cup grated Parmesan cheese
- ¼ cup chopped fresh parsley or basil

1. Place the asparagus and peas in a large bowl. Add the olive oil and ½ teaspoon of kosher salt. Toss to coat. Place the vegetables on the sheet pan.

2. Select BAKE, set temperature to 450°F, and set time to 4 minutes. Select START/PAUSE to begin preheating.

3. Once the unit has preheated, slide the pan into the oven.

4. While the vegetables are cooking, dissolve 1 teaspoon of kosher salt in the water. When cooking is complete, remove the pan from the oven and place the tortellini onto the pan with the vegetables. Pour the salted water over the tortellini. Return the pan to the oven.

5. Select BAKE, set temperature to 450°F, and set time to 7 minutes. Select START/PAUSE to begin.

CONTINUED ▶

6. While the pasta cooks, place the heavy cream in a small bowl. Stir in the garlic and remaining ½ teaspoon of kosher salt.

7. When cooking is complete, remove the pan from the oven and blot off any remaining water with a paper towel. Gently stir the ingredients. Pour the cream over everything and scatter the tomatoes on top.

8. Select AIR ROAST, set temperature to 375°F, and set time to 5 minutes. Select START/PAUSE to begin preheating.

9. Once the unit has preheated, slide the pan into the oven. After 4 minutes, remove the pan from the oven. The tortellini should be tender and the vegetables just barely crisp; if not, cook for 1 minute more.

10. Remove the pan from the oven. Stir in the Parmesan cheese until it's melted (you might find it easier to transfer the mixture to a bowl to do this). Top with the parsley, and serve.

Per serving: *Calories: 662; Total Fat: 39g; Saturated Fat: 21g; Cholesterol: 134mg; Sodium: 757mg; Carbohydrates: 57g; Fiber: 5g; Protein: 25g*

Tilapia Meunière with Green Beans and Potatoes, *page 113*

6

Fish and Seafood Mains

Honey Mustard Salmon with Asparagus

Roasting salmon is a smart way to cook this popular, healthy fish. You don't have to worry about it sticking or breaking up when you turn it, and a quick glaze it all it takes to season it. Asparagus will cook at the same rate as the fish, so it makes a perfect side dish. For best results, look for thick asparagus stalks with tight, dry buds.

DAIRY-FREE OPTION,
GLUTEN-FREE, NUT-FREE,
UNDER 30 MINUTES

PREP TIME: 10 minutes
AIR ROAST: 15 minutes
TOTAL TIME: 25 minutes

SUBSTITUTION:
If asparagus isn't available, substitute trimmed green beans.

4 (6-ounce) salmon fillets, with or without skin

1 teaspoon kosher salt or ½ teaspoon fine salt, divided

1 tablespoon honey

2 teaspoons Dijon mustard

2 tablespoons unsalted butter, melted, or extra-virgin olive oil for dairy-free

2 pounds asparagus, trimmed

Lemon wedges, for serving

1. Sprinkle the salmon on both sides with ½ teaspoon of kosher salt.

2. In a small bowl, whisk together the honey, mustard, and 1 tablespoon of butter.

3. Place the asparagus on the sheet pan. Drizzle with the remaining 1 tablespoon of butter and sprinkle with the remaining ½ teaspoon of salt. Toss to coat. Move the asparagus to the outside of the sheet pan.

4. Pat the salmon dry with a paper towel. Place the fillets on the sheet pan (skin-side down if using skin-on fillets). Brush with the honey mustard sauce.

5. Select AIR ROAST, set temperature to 375ºF, and set time to 15 minutes. Select START/PAUSE to begin preheating.

6. Once the oven has preheated, slide the pan into the oven.

7. After 7 to 8 minutes, remove the pan from the oven and toss the asparagus. Return the pan to the oven and continue cooking.

8. When cooking is complete, remove the pan from the oven. Place the salmon and asparagus on plate. Squeeze a little lemon juice over the fish and vegetables, and serve.

Per serving: *Calories: 495; Total Fat: 34g; Saturated Fat: 7g; Cholesterol: 93mg; Sodium: 267mg; Carbohydrates: 16g; Fiber: 6g; Protein: 36g*

Oven-Roasted Shrimp "Boil"

SERVES 4

This oven version of the famous shrimp boil (called Frogmore stew in the Southeast) is less messy and, I think, much tastier than the traditional boil, which tends to dilute the flavor of the ingredients. Adding the ingredients in stages lets the potatoes and corn cook through without overcooking the shrimp.

NUT-FREE, GLUTEN-FREE, UNDER 30 MINUTES

PREP TIME: 10 time
AIR ROAST: 15 minutes
TOTAL TIME: 25 minutes

DID YOU KNOW: Old Bay is the brand name of a moderately spicy seasoning that originated in the Chesapeake Bay area. Penzey's Chesapeake seasoning is similar. If you can't find either one, mix together 1½ tablespoons celery salt, ½ teaspoon cayenne pepper, ½ teaspoon freshly ground black pepper, ½ teaspoon paprika, and ½ teaspoon granulated onion or onion powder.

1 pound small red potatoes

2 ears corn, shucked and cut into rounds 1 to 1½ inches thick

½ cup unsalted butter, melted

2 tablespoons Old Bay or similar seasoning

1 (12- to 13-ounce) package kielbasa or other smoked sausages

3 garlic cloves, minced or pressed

1 pound medium (21–25 or 25–30 count) shrimp, peeled and deveined

1. If the potatoes are 2 inches or smaller in diameter, cut them in half. If larger, cut in quarters. Place in a large bowl and add the corn pieces.

2. In a small bowl, mix together the butter and Old Bay seasoning. Drizzle half the butter mixture over the potatoes and corn and toss to coat. Place the vegetables on the sheet pan, reserving the bowl.

3. Select AIR ROAST, set temperature to 350°F, and set time to 15 minutes. Select START/PAUSE to begin preheating.

4. Once the unit has preheated, slide the pan into the oven.

5. While the vegetables cook, cut the sausages into 2-inch lengths, then cut each piece in half lengthwise. Stir the garlic into the remaining butter mixture. Place the shrimp and sausage pieces in the vegetable bowl.

CONTINUED ▶

6. After 10 minutes, remove the pan from the oven. Place the vegetables in the bowl. Pour the garlic butter over and toss to coat. Place the vegetables, sausage, and shrimp on the pan.

7. Return the pan to the oven and continue cooking. After 5 minutes, check the shrimp. They should be pink and opaque. If they are not quite cooked through, return pan to the oven for 1 minute more.

8. When cooking is complete, remove the pan from the oven and serve.

Per serving: *Calories: 643; Total Fat: 40g; Saturated Fat: 20g; Cholesterol: 300mg; Sodium: 1732mg; Carbohydrates: 36g; Fiber: 5g; Protein: 39g*

Roasted Nicoise Salad

Apparently, there's a fair amount of debate about what constitutes an "authentic" Nicoise salad. I first had it with tuna, tomatoes, eggs, olives, new potatoes, and green beans, and that's the way I've always made it. Recently I was told that the potatoes and beans aren't necessary, or even desirable. I didn't listen. I've even taken it a step further, roasting the potatoes, green beans, and cherry tomatoes for extra flavor.

DAIRY-FREE, NUT-FREE, GLUTEN-FREE, UNDER 30 MINUTES

PREP TIME: 10 minutes
AIR ROAST: 15 minutes
TOTAL TIME: 27 minutes

SUBSTITUTION: If you have leftover cooked salmon, it makes a great addition instead of the tuna.

HACK IT: If you have a favorite bottled vinaigrette, you can use it instead of making your own.

- 10 ounces small red potatoes, quartered
- 8 tablespoons extra-virgin olive oil, divided
- 1 teaspoon kosher salt or ½ teaspoon fine salt, divided
- ½ pound green beans, trimmed
- 1 pint cherry tomatoes
- 3 tablespoons red or white wine vinegar
- 1 teaspoon Dijon mustard
- Freshly ground black pepper
- 1 (9-ounce) bag spring greens, washed and dried if necessary
- 2 (5-ounce) cans oil-packed tuna, drained
- 2 hard-cooked eggs, peeled and quartered
- ⅓ cup Nicoise or kalamata olives, pitted

1. Place the potatoes in a large bowl. Drizzle with 1 tablespoon of olive oil and ¼ teaspoon of kosher salt. Place on the sheet pan.

2. Select AIR ROAST, set temperature to 375°F, and set time to 15 minutes. Select START/PAUSE to begin preheating.

3. Once the unit has preheated, slide the pan into the oven.

4. While the potatoes are cooking, place the green beans and cherry tomatoes in the bowl and toss with 1 tablespoon of oil and ¼ teaspoon of kosher salt.

CONTINUED ▶

5. After 10 minutes, remove the pan from the oven. Add the green beans and tomatoes to the pan. Return the pan to the oven and continue cooking.

6. While the vegetables cook, make the vinaigrette: In a small jar or bowl, shake or whisk together the remaining 6 tablespoons of olive oil, vinegar, mustard, the remaining ½ teaspoon of kosher salt, and a few grinds of black pepper.

7. When cooking is complete, remove the pan from the oven. Let the vegetables cool for a few minutes.

8. Arrange the greens on a platter and spoon the tuna into the middle of the greens. Surround the tuna with the potatoes, green beans, tomatoes, and egg quarters. Drizzle with the vinaigrette and scatter the olives on top.

Per serving: *Calories: 502; Total Fat: 37g; Saturated Fat: 6g; Cholesterol: 103mg; Sodium: 558mg; Carbohydrates: 22g; Fiber: 6g; Protein: 24g*

Warm Caesar Salad with Shrimp

SERVES 4

If you've never tried roasted romaine lettuce, you're in for a treat. It's particularly wonderful as the base for a warm Caesar-inspired salad. Roasted shrimp turn it into an easy and elegant dinner. Yes, you can use store-bought croutons, but once you've made your own, you'll never go back.

NUT-FREE, UNDER
30 MINUTES

PREP TIME: 10 minutes
AIR FRY: 4 minutes
AIR ROAST: 9 minutes
TOTAL TIME: 25 minutes

ACCESSORIES:
Air Fry Basket

VARIATION: Try substituting chicken breast for the shrimp. Cut a pound of boneless chicken breasts into 1-inch chunks. Cook for the same amount of time, then check one for doneness. The chicken may take a minute longer.

½ baguette, cut into 1-inch cubes (about 2½ cups)

4 tablespoons extra-virgin olive oil, divided

¼ teaspoon kosher salt or ⅛ teaspoon fine salt

¼ teaspoon granulated garlic

2 romaine lettuce hearts

¾ cup Caesar Dressing (page 200) or store-bought variety, divided

1 pound medium (21–25 or 25–30 count) shrimp, peeled and deveined

2 ounces Parmesan cheese, coarsely grated or shaved (about ⅔ cup)

1. For the croutons, place the bread cubes in a medium bowl. Drizzle with 3 tablespoons of olive oil and sprinkle with the salt and granulated garlic. Toss to coat the bread cubes. Place in the Air Fry basket in a single layer.

2. Select AIR FRY, set temperature to 400°F, and set time to 4 minutes. Select START/PAUSE to begin preheating.

3. Once the unit has preheated, slide the basket into the oven. After about 2 minutes, remove the basket and toss the croutons, reinsert the basket in the oven, and continue cooking. When cooking is complete, the croutons will be crisp and golden brown. Remove the basket from the oven and set aside.

4. While the croutons cook, halve the romaine hearts lengthwise (through the root). Trim the end of the root off, but leave enough to keep the halves intact. Brush the cut side of the lettuce with 2 tablespoons of Caesar Dressing.

5. Place the shrimp in a large bowl and toss with the ¼ cup of Caesar Dressing. Set aside.

6. Brush the sheet pan with the remaining 1 tablespoon of olive oil. Place the romaine halves cut-side down on the pan. Brush the tops with another 2 tablespoons of Caesar Dressing.

7. Select AIR ROAST, set temperature to 375°F, and set time to 10 minutes. Select START/PAUSE to begin preheating.

8. Once the unit has preheated, slide the pan into the oven. After 5 minutes, remove the pan and turn over the romaine halves. Spoon the shrimp around the lettuce. Return the pan to the oven and continue cooking.

9. When cooking is complete, the shrimp should be pink and opaque. If they are not quite cooked through, return pan to the oven for 1 minute more.

10. To serve, place a romaine half on each of four plates. Divide the shrimp among the plates and garnish with croutons and Parmesan cheese.

Per serving: Calories: 651; Total Fat: 46g; Saturated Fat: 8g; Cholesterol: 205mg; Sodium: 1102mg; Carbohydrates: 25g; Fiber: 1g; Protein: 31g

Shrimp with Celery and Toasted Cashews

Shrimp and celery are a surprisingly delicious combination, as this easy Asian-inspired recipe proves. Cashews give the dish roasted flavors and richness. I like my cashews extra toasty for this, so even though I start with roasted salted nuts, I toast them for a couple of minutes in the air fry basket. You can skip that step if you want to save a little time.

DAIRY-FREE, UNDER
30 MINUTES

PREP TIME: 10 minutes
AIR FRY: 2 minutes
AIR ROAST: 8 minutes
TOTAL TIME: 20 minutes

ACCESSORY:
Air Fry Basket

1 cup roasted, salted cashews

½ cup Asian-Style Sauce (page 197)

1 tablespoon sesame oil

½ teaspoon red pepper flakes

1 teaspoon cornstarch

1 tablespoon dry sherry (optional)

1¼ pound medium shrimp (21–25 or 25–30 count), peeled and deveined

6 scallions, thinly sliced, white and green parts separated

8 stalks celery, sliced on the diagonal about ⅓-inch thick

1. Place the cashews in the Air Fry basket.

2. Select AIR FRY, set temperature to 400°F, and set time to 25 minutes. Select START/PAUSE to begin preheating.

3. Once the unit has preheated, slide the basket into the oven. After 1 minute, check the cashews; if they are dark golden brown, remove the basket from the oven. If not, continue cooking for another 30 seconds to 1 minute. Set aside to cool.

4. In a small bowl, mix together the Asian-Style Sauce, sesame oil, red pepper flakes, cornstarch, and sherry (if using).

5. Place the shrimp in a medium bowl. Pour about one-third over the shrimp and toss to coat. Set aside.

6. Place the white parts of the scallions and celery on the sheet pan. Pour the remaining sauce over and toss to coat well.

7. Select AIR ROAST, set temperature to 375°F, and set time to 8 minutes. Select START/PAUSE to begin preheating.

8. Once the unit has preheated, slide the pan into the oven.

9. After 3 minutes, remove the pan from the oven. Add the shrimp and half of the green parts of the scallions to the celery mixture and stir to combine. Return the pan to the oven and finish cooking.

10. When cooking is complete, the shrimp should be pink and opaque. Remove the pan from the oven. Stir in the cashews and garnish with the remaining scallion greens. Serve with steamed rice, if desired.

Per serving: Calories: 383; Total Fat: 21g; Saturated Fat: 4g; Cholesterol: 267mg; Sodium: 600mg; Carbohydrates: 16g; Fiber: 3g; Protein: 35g

Teriyaki Salmon with Baby Bok Choy

SERVES 4

Salmon gets a delicious boost from the salty-sweet flavor of teriyaki sauce in this easy recipe. The mild bitterness of the bok choy, a member of the cabbage family, is a nice complement. If you can't find the baby variety, you can substitute part of a head of regular bok choy, sliced thin.

DAIRY-FREE, NUT-FREE,
UNDER 30 MINUTES

PREP TIME: 15 minutes
AIR ROAST: 15 minutes
TOTAL TIME: 30 minutes

¾ **cup Teriyaki Sauce (page 199) or store-bought variety**

4 **(6-ounce) skinless salmon fillets**

4 **heads baby bok choy, root ends trimmed off and cut in half lengthwise through the root**

1 **tablespoon vegetable oil**

1 **teaspoon sesame oil**

1 **tablespoon toasted sesame seeds**

1. Set aside ¼ cup of Teriyaki Sauce and pour the rest into a resealable plastic bag. Place the salmon in the bag and seal, squeezing as much air out as possible. Let the salmon marinate for at least 10 minutes (longer if you have the time).

2. Place the bok choy halves on the sheet pan. Drizzle the vegetable and sesame oils over the vegetables and toss to coat. Drizzle about a tablespoon of the reserved Teriyaki Sauce over the bok choy, then push them to the sides of the pan.

3. Place the salmon fillets in the middle of the sheet pan.

4. Select AIR ROAST, set temperature to 375°F, and set time to 15 minutes. Select START/PAUSE to begin preheating.

5. Once the unit has preheated, slide the pan into the oven.

6. When cooking is complete, remove the pan from the oven. Brush the salmon with the remaining Teriyaki Sauce. Garnish with the sesame seeds. Serve with steamed rice, if desired.

Per serving: *Calories: 428; Total Fat: 24g; Saturated Fat: 5g; Cholesterol: 97mg; Sodium: 1921mg; Carbohydrates: 14g; Fiber: 2g; Protein: 40g*

Sesame Scallops with Snow Peas and Mushrooms

SERVES 4

Sesame seeds make a delicious crust for sea scallops, and roasting them in the Ninja® Foodi™ Digital Air Fry Oven couldn't be quicker or easier. Snow peas and mushrooms are a nice accompaniment to this elegant yet simple dinner.

DAIRY-FREE, NUT-FREE, UNDER 30 MINUTES

PREP TIME: 10 minutes
AIR ROAST: 8 minutes
TOTAL TIME: 18 minutes

DID YOU KNOW:
Scallops are sometimes treated with a chemical (sodium tripolyphosphate) that helps preserve the scallops and keep moisture in them. There's nothing unsafe about it, but it does make the scallops release a lot of liquid when they cook, which means it's virtually impossible to get a nice crust on them. Look for scallops in the seafood case that are dry and not bright white—it's a good sign if they're beige to a very light orange. If buying frozen scallops, look at the label to see if STPP is an ingredient.

1 pound sea scallops

3 tablespoons hoisin sauce

½ cup toasted sesame seeds

6 ounces snow peas, trimmed

3 teaspoons vegetable oil, divided

1 teaspoon sesame oil

1 teaspoon soy sauce

1 cup Oven-Roasted Mushrooms (page 201)

1. With a basting brush, coat the flat sides of the scallops with the hoisin sauce. Place the sesame seeds in a flat dish. Place the coated sides of the scallops in the seeds, pressing them into the scallops to adhere. Repeat with the other sides of the scallops, so both flat sides are coated with hoisin sauce and sesame seeds.

2. In a medium bowl, toss the snow peas with 1 teaspoon of vegetable oil, the sesame oil, and soy sauce.

3. Brush the sheet pan with the remaining 2 teaspoons of vegetable oil. Place the scallops in the center of the pan. Arrange the snow peas in a single layer around the scallops.

4. Select AIR ROAST, set temperature to 375°F, and set time to 8 minutes. Select START/PAUSE to begin preheating.

5. Once the unit has preheated, slide the pan into the oven.

CONTINUED ▶

6. After 5 minutes, remove the pan from the oven. Using a small spatula, carefully turn the scallops over. Add the mushrooms to the peas and stir to combine. Return the pan to the oven and continue cooking.

7. When cooking is complete, the peas should be sizzling and the scallops just cooked through. Remove the pan from the oven and serve.

Per serving: *Calories: 296; Total Fat: 15g; Saturated Fat: 2g; Cholesterol: 38mg; Sodium: 457mg; Carbohydrates: 16g; Fiber: 4g; Protein: 25g*

Tilapia Meunière with Green Beans and Potatoes

SERVES 4

"Meunière" refers both to a cooking method and a sauce for fish. Traditionally, the fish is dredged in flour and sautéed in butter. It is then served with lemon, parsley, and more butter. This oven-baked version skips the flour, resulting in a light, flavorful dish, with side dishes cooked on the same pan.

NUT-FREE, GLUTEN-FREE,
UNDER 30 MINUTES

PREP TIME: 10 minutes
AIR ROAST: 20 minutes
TOTAL TIME: 30 minutes

SUBSTITUTION: You can use any firm, mild white fish in place of the tilapia—sole, cod, or flounder, for instance.

10 ounces Yukon Gold potatoes, sliced ¼-inch thick

5 tablespoons unsalted butter, melted, divided

1 teaspoon kosher salt or ½ teaspoon fine salt, divided

4 (8-ounce) tilapia fillets

½ pound green beans, trimmed

Juice of 1 lemon

2 tablespoons chopped fresh parsley

1. Place the potatoes in a large bowl. Drizzle with 2 tablespoons of butter and ¼ teaspoon of kosher salt. Place on the sheet pan.

2. Select AIR ROAST, set temperature to 375°F, and set time to 20 minutes. Select START/PAUSE to begin preheating.

3. Once the unit has preheated, slide the pan into the oven.

4. While the potatoes cook, salt the fish fillets on both sides with ½ teaspoon of kosher salt. Place the green beans in the potato bowl and toss with the remaining ¼ teaspoon of kosher salt and 1 tablespoon of butter.

5. After 10 minutes, remove the pan from the oven and move the potatoes to one side. Place the fish fillets in the center of the pan and add the green beans on the other side. Drizzle the fish with 2 tablespoons of butter. Return the pan to the oven and continue cooking.

CONTINUED ▶

Tilapia Meunière with Green Beans and Potatoes _{continued}

6. When cooking is complete, the fish should flake apart with a fork. The beans should be tender and starting to crisp. Remove the pan from the oven. To serve, drizzle the lemon juice over the fish, and sprinkle the parsley over the fish and vegetables.

Per serving: *Calories: 384; Total Fat: 17g; Saturated Fat: 10g; Cholesterol: 149mg; Sodium: 268mg; Carbohydrates: 16g; Fiber: 4g; Protein: 43g*

Snapper Veracruz

The famous Snapper Veracruz is traditionally made with a whole fish, but this version uses fillets for a simple yet delicious weeknight dinner. While it does have several steps, it still comes together quickly. And it's worth the effort, if I do say so myself.

DAIRY-FREE, NUT-FREE, GLUTEN-FREE, UNDER 30 MINUTES

PREP TIME: 9 minutes
AIR ROAST: 18 minutes
TOTAL TIME: 27 minutes

- 2 tablespoons extra-virgin olive oil
- ½ onion, chopped fine (about ½ cup)
- 2 large garlic cloves, minced
- 1 (14.5-ounce) can diced tomatoes, drained
- ½ teaspoon dried oregano
- ¼ cup sliced green olives
- 2 tablespoons chopped fresh parsley, divided
- 3 tablespoons capers, divided
- 4 (6-ounce) snapper fillets
- ½ teaspoon kosher salt or ¼ teaspoon fine salt

1. Pour the olive oil onto the sheet pan. Slide the pan into the oven.

2. Select AIR ROAST, set temperature to 375°F, and set time to 18 minutes. Select START/PAUSE to begin preheating.

3. When unit has preheated, remove the pan from the oven and add the onion and garlic to the oil in the pan. Stir the vegetables to coat with the oil. Return the pan to the oven and continue cooking.

4. After 2 minutes, remove the pan from the oven. Add the tomatoes, oregano, olives, 1 tablespoon of parsley, and 1½ tablespoons of capers. Stir gently to combine. Return the pan to the oven and continue cooking for 6 minutes to heat the sauce through.

5. While the sauce cooks, season the snapper fillets on both sides with the salt.

CONTINUED ▶

6. After 6 minutes, remove the pan from the oven. Place the snapper fillets in the middle of the sheet pan and spoon some of the sauce over the fish. Return the pan to the oven and continue cooking.

7. When cooking is complete, the fish should flake apart with a fork. Remove the pan from the oven and garnish with the remaining 1 tablespoon of parsley and 1½ tablespoons of capers. Serve with steamed rice or warm tortillas, if desired.

Per serving: *Calories: 325; Total Fat: 12g; Saturated Fat: 1g; Cholesterol: 79mg; Sodium: 474mg; Carbohydrates: 8g; Fiber: 3g; Protein: 45g*

Mediterranean Salmon with Tomatoes and Peppers

I love tomatoes with salmon, and this dinner combines the two to delicious effect. If you can find multicolored tomatoes, they make a great presentation, but the red tomatoes are just as tasty. I like to add some toward the end of the cooking, so they keep their shape and texture.

DAIRY-FREE, GLUTEN-FREE, NUT-FREE, UNDER 30 MINUTES

PREP TIME: 10 minutes
AIR ROAST: 15 minutes
TOTAL TIME: 25 minutes

VARIATION: Try adding a small (14- or 15-ounce) can of drained cannellini beans to the tomatoes at step 2.

4 (6-ounce) salmon fillets, with or without skin

1 teaspoon kosher salt or ½ teaspoon fine salt, divided

2 pints cherry or grape tomatoes, halved if large, divided

3 tablespoons extra-virgin olive oil, divided

1 small red bell pepper, seeded and chopped

2 garlic cloves, minced

2 tablespoons chopped fresh basil, divided

1. Sprinkle the salmon on both sides with ½ teaspoon of kosher salt.

2. Place about half of the tomatoes in a large bowl, reserving the remainder. Add the remaining ½ teaspoon of kosher salt, 2 tablespoons of olive oil, the bell pepper, garlic, and 1 tablespoon of basil. Toss to coat the vegetables with the oil. Place the vegetables on the sheet pan.

3. Pat the salmon dry with a paper towel. Place the fillets on the pan (skin-side down). Brush them with the remaining 1 tablespoon of olive oil.

4. Select AIR ROAST, set temperature to 375ºF, and set time to 15 minutes. Select START/PAUSE to begin preheating.

5. Once the unit has preheated, slide the pan into the oven.

CONTINUED ▶

6. After 7 minutes, remove the pan from the oven and add the remaining tomatoes. Return the pan to the oven and continue cooking for about 6 minutes.

7. When cooking is complete, the fish will flake apart with a fork. If the fish is not done, return the pan to the oven for another minute or so. Remove the pan from the oven. Before serving, sprinkle the remaining 1 tablespoon of basil over the dish.

Per serving: *Calories: 493; Total Fat: 29g; Saturated Fat: 5g; Cholesterol: 124mg; Sodium: 149mg; Carbohydrates: 12g; Fiber: 2g; Protein: 44g*

White Clam Pizza

SERVES 4

I haven't ever tried the "original" clam pizza from New Haven, Connecticut, so I don't know how this one compares. But I like it; it's a tasty change from our regular tomato sauced pizzas. If you can find fresh shucked or frozen clams, they're a great upgrade; just add them when the pizza first goes into the oven.

NUT-FREE, UNDER 30 MINUTES

PREP TIME: 15 minutes
AIR ROAST: 12 minutes
TOTAL TIME: 30 minutes

VARIATION: If you and your family aren't clam fans, you can leave them off and substitute a little smoked salmon or trout.

¼ cup extra-virgin olive oil, plus a little extra for forming the crust

2 large garlic cloves, chopped

¼ teaspoon red pepper flakes

1 pound store-bought pizza dough

½ cup shredded mozzarella cheese (4 ounces)

2 (6.5-ounce) cans chopped clams, drained

¼ cup grated Parmesan cheese

½ cup coarsely chopped fresh parsley

2 teaspoons chopped fresh oregano (optional)

1. In a small bowl, whisk together the olive oil with the garlic and red pepper flakes. Let it sit while you work on the dough.

2. Punch down the pizza dough to release as much air as possible. Place the dough on the sheet pan and press it out toward the edges. The dough will likely spring back and shrink. Be patient and keep working at it, leaving it to relax for a few minutes from time to time. As it stretches, I find it helpful to coat my fingers with some olive oil and then poke the dough lightly with my fingertips to keep it from shrinking as much. Don't worry if you can't get it all the way to the edges of the pan.

3. Brush half of the garlic oil over the dough. Evenly distribute the mozzarella cheese over the dough.

4. Select AIR ROAST, set temperature to 425°F, and set time to 12 minutes. Select START/PAUSE to begin preheating.

5. Once the unit has preheated, slide the pan into the oven.

6. After about 8 minutes, remove the pan from the oven. Scatter the clams over the pizza and sprinkle the Parmesan cheese on top. Return the pan to the oven and continue cooking for another 4 to 6 minutes. If you like a crisp crust, you can use a pizza peel or cake lifter (or even a very large spatula) to slide the pizza off the pan and directly onto the rack.

7. When cooking is complete, the cheese on top is lightly browned and bubbling and the crust is deep golden brown. Remove the pan from the oven (if you haven't already). Place the pizza on a wire rack to cool for a few minutes (a rack will keep the crust from getting soggy as it cools). Sprinkle the parsley and oregano (if using) over the pizza and drizzle with the remaining garlic oil. Slice and serve.

Per serving: *Calories: 570; Total Fat: 26g; Saturated Fat: 7g; Cholesterol: 78mg; Sodium: 608mg; Carbohydrates: 53g; Fiber: 4g; Protein: 36g*

Southwestern Chicken Skewers with Corn Salad, *page 124*

7

Poultry Mains

Southwestern Chicken Skewers with Corn Salad

Who says you need a grill for skewers? They're easy and just as tasty made in the oven. Get your kids to help assemble the skewers, and they'll be done before you know it. This recipe pairs Southwestern-style chicken and vegetables with a delicious Mexican corn salad known as esquites.

NUT-FREE, GLUTEN-FREE, UNDER 30 MINUTES

PREP TIME: 17 minutes
AIR ROAST: 10 minutes
TOTAL TIME: 27 minutes

ACCESSORIES: 12 (9- to 12-inch) wooden skewers, soaked in water for at least 30 minutes

DID YOU KNOW: *Elotes,* or Mexican street corn, is roasted corn on the cob that's spread with mayonnaise after cooking and sprinkled with chile powder and cotija cheese, which is similar to Parmesan. *Esquites* uses the same ingredients, but with the corn cut off the cob. It can be served warm or at room temperature.

1 pound boneless, skinless chicken breast, cut into 1½-inch chunks

1 large onion, cut into large chunks

1 red bell pepper, seeded and cut into 1-inch pieces

1 green bell pepper, seeded and cut into 1-inch pieces

3 tablespoons vegetable oil, divided

2 tablespoons Southwestern Seasoning (page 206) or store-bought southwestern or fajita seasoning

2 teaspoons kosher salt or 1 teaspoon fine salt, divided

2 cups corn, fresh or frozen, thawed and drained

¼ teaspoon granulated garlic

1 tablespoon mayonnaise

1 teaspoon freshly squeezed lime juice

3 tablespoons grated Parmesan cheese

1. Place the chicken, onion, and bell peppers in a large bowl. Add 2 tablespoons of oil, the Southwestern Seasoning, and 1½ teaspoons of kosher salt (omit if using a store-bought seasoning mix that includes salt). Toss to coat evenly.

2. Alternate the chicken and vegetables on the skewers, making about 12 skewers (if you use the larger skewers, you'll probably only need 8).

3. Place the corn in a medium bowl, and add the remaining 1 tablespoon of oil. Add the remaining ½ teaspoon of kosher salt and the garlic, and toss to coat. Place the

corn in an even layer on the sheet pan and place the skewers on top.

4. Select AIR ROAST, set temperature to 375°F, and set time to 10 minutes. Select START/PAUSE to begin preheating.

5. Once the unit has preheated, slide the pan into the oven.

6. After about 5 minutes, remove the pan from the oven and turn the skewers. Return the pan to the oven and continue cooking.

7. When cooking is complete, remove the pan from the oven. Place the skewers on a platter and cover with aluminum foil to stay warm. Place the corn back into the bowl and add the mayonnaise, lime juice, and Parmesan cheese. Stir to combine.

Per serving: Calories: 356; Total Fat: 17g; Saturated Fat: 3g; Cholesterol: 79mg; Sodium: 313mg; Carbohydrates: 24g; Fiber: 4g; Protein: 30g

Braised Chicken with Polenta

SERVES 4

This recipe, also known as Chicken Scarpariello, *is a classic Italian American dish of braised chicken and sausages with fresh and pickled peppers. My version takes it to the Ninja® Foodi™ Digital Air Fry Oven, so it's done faster, and adds polenta, so it's a one-dish meal. I like the sausage as an accent, but feel free to add another link or two if you like more.*

DAIRY-FREE, NUT-FREE, GLUTEN-FREE

PREP TIME: 10 minutes
AIR ROAST: 27 minutes
TOTAL TIME: 37 minutes

VARIATION: The combination of fresh and pickled peppers is delicious with all kinds of meats—you can increase the number of sausages and leave the chicken out entirely, or use the peppers and onion as a side dish for pork chops or pork tenderloin.

4 bone-in, skin-on chicken thighs (about 1½ pounds)

1½ teaspoon kosher salt or ¾ teaspoon fine salt, divided

Cooking oil spray

1 link sweet or hot Italian sausage (about ¼ pound), whole

8 ounces miniature bell peppers, halved and seeded (or 1 large red bell pepper, thinly sliced)

1 small onion, thinly sliced

2 garlic cloves, minced

1 tablespoon extra-virgin olive oil

4 hot or sweet pickled cherry peppers, seeded and quartered, along with 2 tablespoons pickling liquid from the jar

¼ cup low-sodium chicken stock

4 (1-inch) slices Oven Polenta (page 204)

1. Salt the chicken thighs on both sides with 1 teaspoon of kosher salt. Spray the sheet pan with cooking oil spray and place the thighs skin-side down on the pan. Add the sausage.

2. Select AIR ROAST, set temperature to 375ºF, and set time to 27 minutes. Select START/PAUSE to begin preheating.

3. Once the unit has preheated, slide the pan into the oven.

4. While the chicken and sausage cook, place the bell peppers, onion, and garlic in a large bowl. Sprinkle with the remaining ½ teaspoon of kosher salt and add the olive oil. Toss to coat.

5. After 10 minutes, remove the pan from the oven and turn over the chicken thighs and sausage. Add the pepper mixture to the pan. Return the pan to the oven and continue cooking.

6. After another 10 minutes, remove the pan from the oven and add the pickled peppers, pickling liquid, and stock. Stir the pickled peppers into the peppers and onion. Push them to the side and add the polenta slices in a single layer. Return the pan to the oven and continue cooking.

7. When cooking is complete, the peppers and onion should be soft, the polenta warmed through, and the chicken should read 165°F on a meat thermometer. Remove the pan from the oven. Slice the sausage into thin pieces and stir it into the pepper mixture. Place a slice of polenta on each of four plates and spoon the peppers over. Top with a chicken thigh.

Per serving: *Calories: 513; Total Fat: 37g; Saturated Fat: 10g; Cholesterol: 163mg; Sodium: 550mg; Carbohydrates: 10g; Fiber: 2g; Protein: 35g*

Chicken Parm Sandwiches on Ciabatta

SERVES 4

Chicken Parmesan (or Chicken Parm if you want to be trendy) is an Italian American favorite. Making it in the Ninja® Foodi™ Digital Air Fry Oven is a lot less messy than the traditional stovetop and oven method. I like it best in a sandwich, with a little marinara sauce and lots of gooey cheese.

NUT-FREE, UNDER
30 MINUTES

PREP TIME: 12 minutes
AIR FRY: 10 minutes
AIR BROIL: 3 minutes
TOTAL TIME: 25 minutes

ACCESSORIES:
Air Fry Basket

VARIATION: If you like, skip the buns and serve the chicken Parm plain or with pasta. Just place the chicken pieces on the sheet pan after air frying, spoon the marinara over the pieces, then top with the cheeses. Broil until the cheese melts.

- 2 (8-ounce) boneless, skinless chicken breasts
- 1 teaspoon kosher salt or ½ teaspoon fine salt, divided
- 1 cup all-purpose flour
- 1 teaspoon Italian seasoning or ½ teaspoon each dried oregano and dried basil
- 2 large eggs
- 2 tablespoons plain yogurt
- 2 cups panko bread crumbs
- 1⅓ cups grated Parmesan cheese, divided
- 2 tablespoons extra-virgin olive oil
- 4 ciabatta rolls or other sturdy buns, split in half
- ½ cup Marinara Sauce (page 195) or store-bought variety
- ½ cup shredded mozzarella cheese

1. Lay the chicken breasts on a cutting board and cut each one in half parallel to the board so that you have 4 fairly even, flat fillets. Place a piece of plastic wrap over the chicken pieces and use a rolling pin or small skillet to gently pound them to an even thickness, about ½-inch thick. Season the chicken on both sides with ½ teaspoon of kosher salt.

2. Place the flour on a plate and add the remaining ½ teaspoon of kosher salt and the Italian seasoning. Mix with a fork to distribute evenly. In a wide bowl, whisk together the eggs with the yogurt. In a small bowl combine the panko, 1 cup of Parmesan cheese, and olive oil. Place this in a shallow bowl or plate.

3. Lightly dredge both sides of the chicken pieces in the seasoned flour, and then dip them in the egg wash to coat completely, letting the excess drip off. Finally, dredge the chicken in the bread crumbs. Carefully place the breaded chicken pieces in the Air Fry basket.

4. Select AIR FRY, set temperature to 375ºF, and set time to 10 minutes. Select START/PAUSE to begin preheating.

5. Once the unit has preheated, slide the basket and sheet pan into the oven.

6. After 5 minutes, remove the basket from the oven. Carefully turn the chicken over. Return the basket to the oven and continue cooking. When cooking is complete, remove the basket and pan from the oven.

7. Open the rolls on the sheet pan, and spread each half with 1 tablespoon of marinara sauce. Place a chicken breast piece on the bottoms of the buns and sprinkle the remaining ⅓ cup of Parmesan cheese over the chicken pieces. Divide the mozzarella among the top halves of the buns.

8. Select AIR BROIL, set temperature to HIGH, and set time to 3 minutes. Select START/PAUSE to begin preheating.

9. Once the unit has preheated, slide the pan into the oven. Check the sandwiches after 2 minutes; when cooking is complete, the mozzarella cheese should be melted and bubbling slightly.

10. Remove the pan from the oven. Close the sandwiches and serve. Add additional marinara sauce if desired.

Per serving: Calories: 710; Total Fat: 25g; Saturated Fat: 9g; Cholesterol: 192mg; Sodium: 738mg; Carbohydrates: 65g; Fiber: 4g; Protein: 55g

Paprika Chicken Thighs with Toasted Slaw

SERVES 4

The cabbage in this recipe ends up halfway between coleslaw and braised cabbage, and it pairs beautifully with the crispy, paprika-spiced chicken thighs. The smoked paprika adds great flavor, but regular paprika is tasty as well.

DAIRY-FREE, NUT-FREE, GLUTEN-FREE

PREP TIME: 10 minutes
AIR ROAST: 27 minutes
TOTAL TIME: 37 minutes

VARIATION: You can use any spice mixture you like in place of the paprika mixture. If the mixture contains salt, reduce the amount of salt you use on the chicken in step 1.

- **4 bone-in, skin-on chicken thighs**
- **1½ teaspoon kosher salt or ¾ teaspoon fine salt, divided**
- **1 tablespoon smoked or sweet paprika**
- **½ teaspoon granulated garlic**
- **½ teaspoon dried oregano**
- **¼ teaspoon freshly ground black pepper**
- **Cooking oil spray**
- **3 cups shredded cabbage or coleslaw mix**
- **½ small red or white onion, thinly sliced**
- **4 large radishes, julienned (optional)**
- **3 tablespoons red or white wine vinegar**
- **2 tablespoons extra-virgin olive oil**

1. Salt the chicken thighs on both sides with 1 teaspoon of kosher salt. In a small bowl, combine the paprika, garlic, oregano, and black pepper. Sprinkle half this mixture over the skin sides of the thighs. Spray the sheet pan with cooking oil spray and place the thighs skin-side down on the pan. Sprinkle the remaining spice mixture over the other sides of the chicken pieces.

2. Select AIR ROAST, set temperature to 375°F, and set time to 27 minutes. Select START/PAUSE to begin preheating.

3. Once the unit has preheated, slide the pan into the oven.

CONTINUED ▶

4. After 10 minutes, remove the pan from the oven and turn over the chicken thighs. Return the pan to the oven and continue cooking.

5. While the chicken cooks, place the cabbage, onion, and radishes (if using) in a large bowl. Sprinkle with the remaining ½ teaspoon of kosher salt, vinegar, and olive oil. Toss to coat.

6. After another 9 to 10 minutes, remove the pan from the oven and place the chicken thighs on a cutting board or plate. Place the cabbage mixture on the pan and toss it with the chicken fat and spices on the bottom of the pan. Spread out the cabbage into an even layer and place the chicken on it, skin-side up. Return the pan to the oven and continue cooking. Roast for another 7 to 8 minutes.

7. When cooking is complete, the cabbage is just becoming tender. Remove the pan from the oven. Taste and adjust the seasoning if necessary. Serve.

Per serving: *Calories: 379; Total Fat: 29g; Saturated Fat: 8g; Cholesterol: 105mg; Sodium: 189mg; Carbohydrates: 14g; Fiber: 2g; Protein: 19g*

Sweet-and-Spicy Drumsticks with Garlic Green Beans

SERVES 4

Thai sweet chili sauce is one of my favorite condiments—sweet, spicy, and just a bit tangy. It makes an easy and delicious glaze for chicken drumsticks. Roasted green beans with lots of garlic make a great accompaniment.

DAIRY-FREE, NUT-FREE, GLUTEN-FREE, 5-INGREDIENT, UNDER 30 MINUTES

PREP TIME: 5 minutes
AIR ROAST: 25 minutes
TOTAL TIME: 30 minutes

VARIATION: In place of the chili sauce, try honey mustard as a glaze for the drumsticks.

8 skin-on chicken drumsticks

1 teaspoon kosher salt or ½ teaspoon fine salt, divided

1 pound green beans, trimmed

2 garlic cloves, minced

2 tablespoons vegetable oil

⅓ cup Thai sweet chili sauce

1. Salt the drumsticks on all sides with ½ teaspoon of kosher salt. Let sit for a few minutes, then blot dry with a paper towel. Place on the sheet pan.

2. Select AIR ROAST, set temperature to 375°F, and set time to 25 minutes. Select START/PAUSE to begin preheating.

3. Once preheated, slide the pan into the oven.

4. While the chicken cooks, place the green beans in a large bowl. Add the remaining ½ teaspoon kosher salt, the garlic, and oil. Toss to coat.

5. After 15 minutes, remove the pan from the oven. Brush the drumsticks with the sweet chili sauce. Place the green beans on the pan. Return the pan to the oven and continue cooking.

6. When cooking is complete, the green beans should be sizzling and browned in spots and the chicken cooked through, reading 165°F on a meat thermometer. Serve the chicken with the green beans on the side.

Per serving: Calories: 288; Total Fat: 15g; Saturated Fat: 1g; Cholesterol: 75mg; Sodium: 677mg; Carbohydrates: 18g; Fiber: 4g; Protein: 20g

Creamy Chicken and Gnocchi

SERVES 4

Gnocchi are Italian potato dumplings. They're time-consuming to make, but fortunately, you can find them premade in the pasta section of the store. In this recipe, they're tossed in a tomato-cream sauce with chicken and spinach for an elegant one-pan meal.

NUT-FREE, UNDER
30 MINUTES

PREP TIME: 10 minutes
BAKE: 7 minutes
AIR ROAST: 6 minutes
TOTAL TIME: 25 minutes

HACK IT: If you can find sun-dried tomato purée with garlic, you can use that and skip smashing a clove.

1 (1-pound) package shelf-stable gnocchi

1¼ cups low-sodium chicken stock

½ teaspoon kosher salt or ¼ teaspoon fine salt

1 pound chicken breast, cut into 1-inch chunks

1 cup heavy (whipping) cream

2 tablespoons sun-dried tomato purée

1 garlic clove, minced or smashed

1 cup frozen spinach, thawed and drained

1 cup grated Parmesan cheese

1. Place the gnocchi in an even layer on the sheet pan. Pour the chicken stock over the gnocchi.

2. Select BAKE, set temperature to 450°F, and set time to 7 minutes. Select START/PAUSE to begin preheating.

3. Once the unit has preheated, slide the pan into the oven.

4. While the gnocchi are cooking, sprinkle the salt over the chicken pieces. In a small bowl, mix together the cream, tomato purée, and garlic.

5. When cooking is complete, blot off any remaining stock, or drain the gnocchi and return it to the pan. Top the gnocchi with the spinach and chicken. Pour the cream mixture over the ingredients on the pan.

6. Select AIR ROAST, set temperature to 400°F, and set time to 6 minutes. Select START/PAUSE to begin preheating.

7. Once the unit has preheated, slide the pan into the oven.

8. After 4 minutes, remove the pan from the oven and gently stir the ingredients. Return the pan to the oven and continue cooking.

9. When cooking is complete, the gnocchi should be tender and the chicken should be cooked through. Remove the pan from the oven. Stir in the Parmesan cheese until it's melted, and serve.

Per serving: *Calories: 789; Total Fat: 32g; Saturated Fat: 18g; Cholesterol: 102mg; Sodium: 1650mg; Carbohydrates: 108g; Fiber: 16g; Protein: 32g*

Sweet-and-Sour Chicken

Traditionally, this Chinese American classic is made with deep-fried chicken. As good as that can be, this version is lighter, just as tasty, and way easier to make at home. If you can find fresh pineapple chunks in the produce section, they're the best choice for the dish; if not, buy pineapple chunks canned in natural juices, not heavy syrup.

DAIRY-FREE, NUT-FREE, UNDER 30 MINUTES

PREP TIME: 10 minutes
AIR ROAST: 10 minutes
TOTAL TIME: 20 minutes

SUBSTITUTION: You can substitute pork tenderloin, cut into the same-size chunks, for the chicken.

1½ pounds boneless, skinless chicken breasts, cut into 1-inch chunks

¾ cup Asian-Style Sauce (page 197)

2 tablespoons ketchup

2 tablespoons brown sugar

2 tablespoons rice vinegar

1 red bell pepper, cut into 1-inch chunks

1 green bell pepper, cut into 1-inch chunks

6 scallions, cut into 1-inch pieces

Cooking oil spray

1 cup (¾-inch chunks) fresh or canned, drained pineapple

1. Place the chicken in a large bowl. Add the Asian-Style Sauce, ketchup, brown sugar, vinegar, red and green peppers, and scallions. Toss to coat.

2. Spray the sheet pan with cooking oil spray and place the chicken and vegetables on the pan.

3. Select AIR ROAST, set temperature to 375ºF, and set time to 10 minutes. Select START/PAUSE to begin preheating.

4. Once the unit has preheated, slide the pan into the oven.

5. After 6 minutes, remove the pan from the oven. Add the pineapple chunks to the pan and stir. Return the pan to the oven and continue cooking.

6. When cooking is complete, remove the pan from the oven. Serve with steamed rice, if desired.

Per serving: Calories: 312; Total Fat: 3g; Saturated Fat: 0g; Cholesterol: 100mg; Sodium: 676mg; Carbohydrates: 24g; Fiber: 2g; Protein: 44g

Curried Chicken and Sweet Potatoes

SERVES 4

There was a time, many years ago, when I put curry powder in pretty much everything I cooked. While that curry powder bears no relation to true Indian curries, it didn't matter to me. I still like it, although I use much less of it these days. It's great with chicken and sweet potatoes, as in this recipe, which also includes Brussels sprouts for a little color and bitterness to offset the sweetness of the potatoes.

NUT-FREE, GLUTEN-FREE, 5-INGREDIENT, UNDER 30 MINUTES

PREP TIME: 10 minutes
AIR ROAST: 20 minutes
TOTAL TIME: 30 minutes

1 pound boneless, skinless chicken thighs

1 teaspoon kosher salt or ½ teaspoon fine salt, divided

¼ cup unsalted butter, melted

1 tablespoon curry powder

2 medium sweet potatoes, peeled and cut in 1-inch cubes

12 ounces Brussels sprouts, halved

1. Salt the chicken thighs with ½ teaspoon of kosher salt. Place them in the center of the sheet pan.

2. In a small bowl, stir together the butter and curry powder.

3. Place the sweet potatoes and Brussels sprouts in a large bowl. Drizzle half the curry butter over the vegetables and add the remaining ½ teaspoon of kosher salt. Toss to coat. Transfer the vegetables to the sheet pan and arrange in a single layer around the chicken. Brush half of the remaining curry butter over the chicken.

4. Select AIR ROAST, set temperature to 400°F, and set time to 20 minutes. Select START/PAUSE to begin preheating.

5. Once the unit has preheated, slide the pan into the oven.

6. After 10 minutes, remove the pan from the oven and turn over the chicken thighs. Baste them with the remaining curry butter. Return the pan to the oven and continue cooking.

7. Cooking is complete when the sweet potatoes are tender and the chicken is cooked through and reads 165°F on a meat thermometer.

Per serving: *Calories: 330; Total Fat: 17g; Saturated Fat: 8g; Cholesterol: 126mg; Sodium: 290mg; Carbohydrates: 22g; Fiber: 6g; Protein: 26g*

Oven-Fried Chicken with Smashed Potatoes and Corn

SERVES 4

Is there any more iconic Sunday dinner than fried chicken and mashed potatoes? When I was growing up, my Mom added corn to that combination—on the cob during the summer, when my Dad always had a big garden. This recipe brings those favorites together again, but cooks them all at once on one pan. Much less messy, and still delicious.

NUT-FREE, FAMILY FAVORITE

PREP TIME: 10 minutes
AIR ROAST: 25 minutes
TOTAL TIME: 35 minutes

SUBSTITUTION: If fresh corn isn't in season, use asparagus or green beans instead. Add to the pan for the last 10 to 12 minutes.

4 bone-in, skin-on chicken thighs

2 teaspoons kosher salt or 1 teaspoon fine salt, divided

1 cup Bisquick or similar baking mix

½ cup unsalted butter, melted, divided

1 pound small red potatoes, quartered

3 ears corn, shucked and cut into rounds 1- to 1½-inches thick

⅓ cup heavy (whipping) cream

½ teaspoon freshly ground black pepper

1. Sprinkle the chicken on all sides with 1 teaspoon of kosher salt. Place the baking mix in a shallow dish. Brush the thighs on all sides with ¼ cup of butter, then dredge them in the baking mix, coating them all on sides. Place the chicken in the center of the sheet pan.

2. Place the potatoes in a large bowl with 2 tablespoons of butter and toss to coat. Place them on one side of the chicken on the pan.

3. Place the corn in a medium bowl and drizzle with the remaining 2 tablespoons of butter. Sprinkle with ¼ teaspoon of kosher salt and toss to coat. Place on the pan on the other side of the chicken.

4. Select AIR ROAST, set temperature to 375°F, and set time to 25 minutes. Select START/PAUSE to begin preheating.

CONTINUED ▶

5. Once the unit has preheated, slide the pan into the oven.

6. After 20 minutes, remove the pan from the oven and transfer the potatoes back to the bowl. Return the pan to oven and continue cooking.

7. As the chicken continues cooking, add the cream, black pepper, and remaining ¾ teaspoon of kosher salt to the potatoes. Lightly mash the potatoes with a potato masher or fork.

8. When cooking is complete, the corn will be tender and the chicken cooked through, reading 165ºF on a meat thermometer. Remove the pan from the oven and serve the chicken with the smashed potatoes and corn on the side.

Per serving: Calories: 763; Total Fat: 55g; Saturated Fat: 27g; Cholesterol: 187mg; Sodium: 429mg; Carbohydrates: 48g; Fiber: 4g; Protein: 24g

Chicken Shawarma with Roasted Tomatoes

If you don't live in a big city where you can get shawarma from a street cart, this is the next best thing. The recipe does have a couple of steps, but you can marinate the chicken while the pitas warm, and then make the sauce while the chicken cooks, so the total time isn't all that long. And it's definitely worth it.

NUT-FREE, UNDER
30 MINUTES

PREP TIME: 10 minutes
BAKE: 6 minutes
AIR BROIL: 12 minutes
TOTAL TIME: 28 minutes

VARIATION: For a
simpler (and gluten-free)
variation, skip the sauce
and pitas, and serve the
chicken and tomatoes
with steamed rice.

1½ pounds boneless,
  skinless chicken thighs

1¼ teaspoon kosher
  salt or ⅜ teaspoon
  fine salt, divided

2 tablespoons plus
  1 teaspoon extra-virgin
  olive oil, divided

⅔ cup plus 2 tablespoons
  plain Greek
  yogurt, divided

2 tablespoons freshly
  squeezed lemon juice
  (about 1 medium lemon)

4 garlic cloves, pressed
  or minced, divided

1 generous tablespoon
  Shawarma Seasoning
  (page 207)

4 pita breads, cut in half

1 pint cherry tomatoes

½ small cucumber

1 tablespoon chopped
  fresh parsley

1. Sprinkle the chicken thighs on both sides with 1 teaspoon of kosher salt. Place in a resealable plastic bag and set aside while you make the marinade.

2. In a small bowl, mix together 2 tablespoons of olive oil, 2 tablespoons of yogurt, the lemon juice, 3 pressed garlic cloves, and Shawarma Seasoning until thoroughly combined. Pour the marinade over the chicken. Seal the bag, squeezing out as much air as possible. and massage the chicken to coat the it with the sauce. Set aside.

3. Wrap 2 pita breads each in two pieces of aluminum foil and place on the sheet pan.

4. Select BAKE, set temperature to 300ºF, and set time to 6 minutes. Select START/PAUSE to begin preheating.

5. Once the oven has preheated, slide the pan into the oven. After 3 minutes, remove the pan from the oven and turn over the foil packets. Return the pan to the oven and continue cooking. When cooking is complete, remove the pan from the oven and place the foil-wrapped pitas on the top of the oven to keep warm.

6. Remove the chicken from the marinade, letting the excess drip off into the bag. Place them on the sheet pan. Arrange the tomatoes around the sides of the chicken. Discard the marinade.

7. Select AIR BROIL, set temperature to HIGH, and set time to 12 minutes. Select START/PAUSE to begin preheating.

8. Once the unit has preheated, slide the pan into the oven.

9. After 6 minutes, remove the pan from the oven and turn over the chicken. Return the pan to the oven and continue cooking.

10. While the chicken cooks, peel and seed the cucumber. Grate or finely chop it. Wrap it in a paper towel to remove as much moisture as possible. Place the cucumber in a small bowl. Add the remaining ⅔ cup of yogurt, ¼ teaspoon kosher salt, 1 teaspoon of olive oil, 1 pressed garlic clove, and parsley. Whisk until combined.

11. When cooking is complete, the chicken should be browned, crisp along its edges, and sizzling. Remove the pan from the oven and place the chicken on a cutting board. Cut each thigh into several pieces. Unwrap the pitas. Spread a tablespoon or two of sauce into a pita half. Add some chicken and add 2 or 3 roasted tomatoes. Serve.

Per serving: Calories: 425; Total Fat: 19g; Saturated Fat: 5g; Cholesterol: 155mg; Sodium: 419mg; Carbohydrates: 25g; Fiber: 2g; Protein: 39g

Turkey Burgers with Cheddar and Roasted Onions

SERVES 4

Turkey burgers can be anything but dry and tasteless. It's just a matter of what you add. Mayonnaise provides fat—which means more flavor and moisture—and also helps bind the meat together. Tangy mustard further spikes the flavor, and Worcestershire sauce ups the umami. Finally, roasted onions and cheese are the perfect complements.

NUT-FREE, FAMILY FAVORITE

PREP TIME: 10 minutes
AIR ROAST: 10 minutes
AIR BROIL: 15 minutes
TOTAL TIME: 35 minutes

- 2 medium yellow or white onions
- 1 tablespoon extra-virgin olive oil or vegetable oil
- 1½ teaspoons kosher salt or ¾ teaspoon fine salt, divided
- 1¼ pound ground turkey
- ⅓ cup mayonnaise
- 1 tablespoon Dijon mustard
- 2 teaspoons Worcestershire sauce
- 4 slices sharp cheddar cheese (about 4 ounces total)
- 4 hamburger buns, sliced

1. Trim the onions and cut them in half through the root. Cut one of the halves in half (so you have a quarter). Grate one quarter. Place the grated onion in a large bowl. Thinly slice the remaining onions and place in a medium bowl with the oil and ½ teaspoon of kosher salt. Toss to coat. Place the onions on the sheet pan in a single layer.

2. Select AIR ROAST, set temperature to 350°F, and set time to 10 minutes. Select START/PAUSE to begin preheating.

3. Once the unit has preheated, slide the pan into the oven.

4. While the onions are cooking, add the turkey to the grated onion. Add the remaining 1 teaspoon of kosher salt, mayonnaise, mustard, and Worcestershire sauce. Mix just until combined, being careful not to overwork the turkey. Divide the mixture into 4 patties, each about ¾-inch thick.

CONTINUED ▶

5. When cooking is complete, remove the pan from the oven. Move the onions to one side of the pan and place the burgers on the pan. Poke your finger into the center of each burger to make a deep indentation (this helps the burgers cook evenly).

6. Select AIR BROIL, set temperature to HIGH, and set time to 12 minutes. Select START/PAUSE to begin preheating.

7. Once preheated, slide the pan into the oven. After 6 minutes, remove the pan. Turn the burgers and stir the onions. (If the onions are getting charred, transfer them to a bowl and cover with foil.) Return the pan to the oven and continue cooking. After about 4 minutes, remove the pan and place the cheese slices on the burgers. Return the pan to the oven and continue cooking for about 1 minute, or until the cheese is melted and the center of the burgers has reached at least 160°F on a meat thermometer.

8. When cooking is complete, remove the pan from the oven. Loosely cover the burgers with foil.

9. Lay out the buns, cut-side up, on the oven rack. Select AIR BROIL; set temperature to HIGH, and set time to 3 minutes. Select START/PAUSE to begin. Check the buns after 2 minutes; they should be lightly browned.

10. Remove the buns from the oven. Assemble the burgers and add any condiments you like.

Per serving: *Calories: 579; Total Fat: 33g; Saturated Fat: 11g; Cholesterol: 147mg; Sodium: 678mg; Carbohydrates: 32g; Fiber: 2g; Protein: 36g*

Bacon-Wrapped Turkey Tenderloins with Honey-Balsamic Carrots

SERVES 4

Wrapping turkey tenderloins with bacon helps keep the turkey from drying out and adds a great smoky flavor. The glazed carrots make a wonderful side, and the honey-balsamic glaze does double duty as a basting sauce for the turkey.

DAIRY-FREE, GLUTEN-FREE, NUT-FREE

PREP TIME: 10 minutes
AIR ROAST: 25 minutes
TOTAL TIME: 35 minutes

DID YOU KNOW:
Turkey tenderloins are often sold "brined," which means that they're injected with a solution of water and salt (and sometimes sugar). This keeps the very lean meat moist and seasons it as well. If the turkey is brined, the label must indicate that fact.

2 (12-ounce) turkey tenderloins

1 teaspoon kosher salt or ½ teaspoon fine salt, divided

6 slices bacon (not thick cut)

3 tablespoons balsamic vinegar

2 tablespoons honey

1 tablespoon Dijon mustard

½ teaspoon dried thyme

6 large carrots, peeled and cut into ¼-inch rounds

1 tablespoon extra-virgin olive oil

1. Sprinkle the turkey with ¾ teaspoon of the salt (if your tenderloins are brined, omit this step). Wrap each tenderloin with 3 strips of bacon, securing the bacon with toothpicks if necessary. Place the turkey on the sheet pan.

2. In a small bowl, mix together the balsamic vinegar, honey, mustard, and thyme.

3. Place the carrots in a medium bowl and drizzle with the oil. Add 1 tablespoon of the balsamic mixture and ¼ teaspoon of kosher salt and toss to coat. Place these on the pan around the turkey tenderloins. Baste the tenderloins with about one-half of the remaining balsamic mixture.

4. Select AIR ROAST, set temperature to 375°F, and set time to 25 minutes. Select START/PAUSE to begin preheating.

CONTINUED ▶

5. Once the unit has preheated, slide the pan into the oven.

6. After 13 minutes, remove the pan from the oven. Gently stir the carrots. Turn over the tenderloins and baste them with the remaining balsamic mixture. Return the pan to the oven and continue cooking.

7. When cooking is complete, the carrots should be tender and the center of the tenderloins should register 155°F on a meat thermometer (the temperature will continue to rise). Remove the pan from the oven. Slice the turkey and serve with the carrots.

Per serving: *Calories: 462; Total Fat: 19g; Saturated Fat: 4g; Cholesterol: 31mg; Sodium: 642mg; Carbohydrates: 20g; Fiber: 3g; Protein: 51g*

Scratch Meatball Subs, *page 166*

8

Beef, Pork, and Lamb Mains

Steak Fajitas

SERVES 4

Fajitas made in the Ninja® Foodi™ Digital Air Fry Oven have a really high reward-to-effort ratio—it's kind of hard to believe that something this tasty can be this easy. It is important to use a fresh spice blend; if you want to make your own, see the recipe for Southwestern Seasoning (page 206).

DAIRY-FREE, GLUTEN-FREE OPTION, UNDER 30 MINUTES

PREP TIME: 10 minutes
BAKE: 6 minutes
AIR ROAST: 9 minutes
TOTAL TIME: 25 minutes

VARIATION: You can use sliced chicken breast or pork tenderloin in place of the steak. The cooking time remains the same.

8 (6-inch) flour or corn tortillas

1 pound top sirloin steak, sliced ¼-inch thick

1 red bell pepper, seeded and sliced ½-inch thick

1 green bell pepper, seeded and sliced ½-inch thick

1 jalapeño, seeded and sliced thin

1 medium onion, sliced ½-inch thick

2 tablespoons vegetable oil

2 tablespoons Mexican seasoning

1 teaspoon kosher salt or ½ teaspoon fine salt

Salsa

1 small avocado, sliced

1. Place a large sheet of aluminum foil on the sheet pan. Place the tortillas on the foil in two stacks and wrap in the foil.

2. Select AIR ROAST, set temperature to 325ºF, and set time to 6 minutes. Select START/PAUSE to begin preheating.

3. Once the unit has preheated, slide the pan into the oven. After 3 minutes, remove the pan from the oven and flip the packet of tortillas over. Return the pan to the oven and continue cooking.

4. While the tortillas warm, place the steak, bell peppers, jalapeño, and onion in a large bowl and drizzle the oil over. Sprinkle with the Mexican seasoning and salt, and toss to coat.

CONTINUED ▶

5. When cooking is complete, remove the pan from the oven and place the packet of tortillas on top of the oven to keep warm. Place the beef and peppers mixture on the sheet pan, spreading out into a single layer as much as possible.

6. Select AIR ROAST, set temperature to 375ºF, and set time to 9 minutes. Select START/PAUSE to begin preheating.

7. Once the unit has preheated, slide the pan into the oven.

8. After about 5 minutes, remove the pan from the oven and stir the ingredients. Return the pan to the oven and continue cooking.

9. When cooking is complete, the vegetables will be soft and browned in places, and the beef will be browned on the outside and barely pink inside. Remove the pan from the oven. Unwrap the tortillas and spoon the fajita mixture into the tortillas. Serve with salsa and avocado slices.

Per serving: *Calories: 348; Total Fat: 23g; Saturated Fat: 5g; Cholesterol: 74mg; Sodium: 453mg; Carbohydrates: 12g; Fiber: 5g; Protein: 23g*

Beef and Crispy Broccoli

SERVES 4

In my recipe for this classic Chinese American dish, I like to give the broccoli a head start by steaming it, so the beef doesn't overcook by the time the broccoli is tender. If you prefer your broccoli browned rather than steamed, just toss it with a little oil and roast it uncovered instead.

DAIRY-FREE, UNDER
30 MINUTES

PREP TIME: 10 minutes
AIR ROAST: 15 minutes
TOTAL TIME: 25 minutes

12 ounces broccoli florets (about 4 cups)

1 pound sirloin or flat iron steak, cut into thin strips

½ teaspoon kosher salt or ¼ teaspoon fine salt

¾ cup Asian-Style Sauce (page 197)

1 teaspoon sriracha or chile-garlic sauce

3 tablespoons freshly squeezed orange juice

1 teaspoon cornstarch

1 medium onion, thinly sliced

1. Place a large piece of aluminum foil on the sheet pan. Place the broccoli on top and sprinkle with 3 tablespoons of water. Seal the broccoli in the foil in a single layer.

2. Select AIR ROAST, set temperature to 375°F, and set time to 6 minutes. Select START/PAUSE to begin preheating.

3. Once the unit has preheated, slide the pan into the oven.

4. While the broccoli steams, sprinkle the steak with the salt. In a small bowl, whisk together the Asian-Style Sauce, sriracha, orange juice, and cornstarch. Place the onion and beef in a large bowl.

5. When cooking is complete, remove the pan from the oven. Open the packet of broccoli and use tongs to transfer the broccoli to the bowl with the beef and onion, discarding the foil and remaining water. Pour the sauce over the beef and vegetables and toss to coat. Place the mixture on the sheet pan.

CONTINUED ▶

6. Select AIR ROAST, set temperature to 375ºF, and set time to 9 minutes. Select START/PAUSE to begin preheating.

7. Once the unit has preheated, slide the pan into the oven.

8. After about 4 minutes, remove the pan from the oven and gently toss the ingredients. Return the pan to oven and continue cooking.

9. When cooking is complete, the sauce should be thickened, the vegetables tender, and the beef barely pink in the center. Serve plain or with steamed rice or Oven Rice (page 203).

Per serving: *Calories: 259; Total Fat: 6g; Saturated Fat: 2g; Cholesterol: 8mg; Sodium: 897mg; Carbohydrates: 20g; Fiber: 3g; Protein: 29g*

Spicy Pork Lettuce Cups

Pork or chicken lettuce cups are usually served as an appetizer in Chinese American restaurants (they were popularized by PF Chang's), but I like them as a main dish. A recipe that allows everyone to assemble their own dinner is my kind of recipe, and it's even better when it's so fast and easy.

DAIRY-FREE, UNDER 30 MINUTES

PREP TIME: 10 minutes
AIR ROAST: 12 minutes
TOTAL TIME: 27 minutes

VARIATION: Boneless chicken thighs can be substituted for the pork tenderloin. Lay them flat on the sheet pan before basting with the sauce, and increase the cooking time by 3 minutes.

- 1 medium pork tenderloin (about 1 pound), silver skin and external fat trimmed
- ⅔ cup Asian-Style Sauce (page 197), divided
- 1 teaspoon cornstarch
- 1 medium jalapeño, seeded and minced
- 1 can diced water chestnuts
- ½ large (or 1 very small) red bell pepper, seeded and chopped
- 2 scallions, chopped, white and green parts separated
- 1 head butter lettuce or Boston lettuce
- ½ cup roasted, chopped almonds or peanuts (optional)
- ¼ cup coarsely chopped cilantro (optional)

1. Cut the tenderloin into ¼-inch slices and place them on the sheet pan. Baste with about 3 tablespoons of Asian-Style Sauce. Stir the cornstarch into the remaining sauce and set aside.

2. Select AIR ROAST, set temperature to 375°F, and set time to 12 minutes. Select START/PAUSE to begin preheating.

3. Once the unit has preheated, slide the pan into the oven.

4. After 5 minutes, remove the pan from the oven. Place the pork slices on a cutting board. Place the jalapeño, water chestnuts, red pepper, and the white parts of the scallions on the sheet pan and pour the remaining sauce over. Stir to coat the vegetables with the sauce. Return the pan to the oven and continue cooking.

CONTINUED ▶

5. While the vegetables cook, chop the pork into small pieces. Separate the lettuce leaves, discarding any tough outer leaves and setting aside the small inner leaves for another use. You'll want 12 to 18 leaves, depending on size and your appetites.

6. After 5 minutes, remove the pan from the oven. Add the pork to the vegetables, stirring to combine. Return the pan to the oven and continue cooking for the remaining 2 minutes, until the pork is warmed back up and the sauce has reduced slightly.

7. When cooking is complete, remove the pan from the oven. Place the pork and vegetables in a medium serving bowl and stir in half the green parts of the scallions. To serve, spoon some of the pork and vegetables into each of the lettuce leaves. Top with the remaining scallion greens and garnish with the nuts and cilantro (if using).

Per serving: *Calories: 216; Total Fat: 6g; Saturated Fat: 2g; Cholesterol: 65mg; Sodium: 175mg; Carbohydrates: 16g; Fiber: 2g; Protein: 21g*

Italian Sausages with Polenta and Grapes

SERVES 6

Grapes might seem like an odd choice to go with sausages, but once I tried the combination, I was hooked. The sweet grapes with a touch of vinegar are the perfect foil for spicy, rich Italian sausage.

NUT-FREE, GLUTEN-FREE, UNDER 30 MINUTES

PREP TIME: 10 minutes
AIR ROAST: 20 minutes
TOTAL TIME: 30 minutes

SUBSTITUTION: If you don't have shallots on hand, thinly sliced red or white onion works fine. Use about ⅓ cup.

2 pounds seedless red grapes

3 shallots, sliced

2 teaspoons fresh thyme or 1 teaspoon dried thyme

2 tablespoons extra-virgin olive oil

½ teaspoon kosher salt or ¼ teaspoon fine salt

Freshly ground black pepper

6 links (about 1½ pounds) hot or sweet Italian sausage

3 tablespoons sherry vinegar or balsamic vinegar

6 (1-inch-thick) slices Oven Polenta (page 204) or store-bought variety

1. Place the grapes in a large bowl. Add the shallots, thyme, olive oil, salt, and pepper. Gently toss. Place the grapes on the sheet pan. Arrange the sausage links evenly on the pan.

2. Select AIR ROAST, set temperature to 375°F, and set time to 20 minutes. Select START/PAUSE to begin preheating.

3. Once preheated, slide the pan into the oven.

4. After 10 minutes, remove the pan. Turn over the sausages and sprinkle the vinegar over the sausages and grapes. Gently toss the grapes and move them to one side of the pan. Place the polenta slices on the pan. Return the pan to the oven and continue cooking.

5. When cooking is complete, the grapes should be very soft and the sausages browned.

Per serving: Calories: 681; Total Fat: 48g; Saturated Fat: 18g; Cholesterol: 115mg; Sodium: 1018mg; Carbohydrates: 42g; Fiber: 1g; Protein: 23g

Braised Pork Chops with Squash and Apples

SERVES 4

Pork and apples are a classic combination, and squash is a welcome addition. In this dish, I cook the fruit and vegetables in a little chicken stock, so they braise while the chops cook. This recipe reminds me of winter, although since this version doesn't heat up the kitchen, you can make it all year long.

GLUTEN-FREE, NUT-FREE, UNDER 30 MINUTES

PREP TIME: 15 minutes
AIR ROAST: 13 minutes
TOTAL TIME: 28 minutes

- **4 boneless pork loin chops, ¾- to 1-inch thick**
- **1 teaspoon kosher salt or ½ teaspoon fine salt, divided**
- **2 tablespoons Dijon mustard**
- **2 tablespoons brown sugar**
- **1 pound butternut squash, cut into 1-inch cubes**
- **1 large Gala or Braeburn apple, peeled and cut into 12 to 16 wedges**
- **1 medium onion, thinly sliced**
- **½ teaspoon dried thyme**
- **¼ teaspoon freshly ground black pepper**
- **1 tablespoon unsalted butter, melted**
- **½ cup low-sodium chicken stock**

1. Sprinkle the pork chops on both sides with ½ teaspoon of kosher salt. In a small bowl, whisk together the mustard and brown sugar. Baste about half of the mixture on one side of the pork chops. Place the chops, basted-side up, on the sheet pan.

2. Place the squash in a large bowl. Add the apple, onion, thyme, remaining ½ teaspoon of kosher salt, pepper, and butter and toss to coat. Arrange the squash-fruit mixture around the chops on the pan. Pour the chicken stock over the mixture, avoiding the chops.

3. Select AIR ROAST, set temperature to 350ºF, and set time to 13 minutes. Select START/PAUSE to begin preheating.

4. Once the unit has preheated, slide the pan into the oven.

5. After about 7 minutes, remove the pan from the oven. Gently toss the squash mixture and turn over the chops. Baste the chops with the remaining mustard mixture. Return the pan to the oven and continue cooking.

6. When cooking is complete, the pork chops should register at least 145°F in the center on a meat thermometer, and the squash and apples should be tender. If necessary, continue cooking for up to 3 minutes more.

7. Remove the pan from the oven. Spoon the squash and apples onto four plates, and place a pork chop on top. If you like, sprinkle with a little fresh thyme or parsley.

Per serving: Calories: 360; Total Fat: 17g; Saturated Fat: 7g; Cholesterol: 63mg; Sodium: 507mg; Carbohydrates: 30g; Fiber: 5g; Protein: 27g

Scratch Meatball Subs

Making meatballs from scratch does take a little time, but these are so good they're worth the effort. Cooking them in the Ninja® Foodi™ Digital Air Fry Oven cuts way down on the mess, and you can make them ahead of time and then assemble the sandwiches when you're ready to eat. Just reheat the meatballs for 10 minutes or so before assembling the sandwiches.

NUT-FREE, FAMILY FAVORITE

PREP TIME: 15 minutes
AIR ROAST: 20 minutes
AIR BROIL: 4 minutes
TOTAL TIME: 39 minutes

1 large egg

¼ cup whole milk

24 saltines, crushed but not pulverized

1 pound ground chuck

1 pound Italian sausage, casings removed

4 tablespoons grated Parmesan cheese, divided

1 teaspoon kosher salt or ½ teaspoon fine salt

4 hoagie or sub rolls, split

1 cup Marinara Sauce (page 195) or store-bought variety

¾ cup shredded mozzarella cheese

1. In a large bowl, whisk the egg into the milk, then stir in the crackers. Let sit for 5 minutes to hydrate.

2. With your hands, break the ground chuck and sausage into the milk mixture, alternating beef and sausage. When you've added half of the meat, sprinkle 2 tablespoons of the grated Parmesan and the salt over it, then continue breaking up the meat until it's all in the bowl. Gently mix everything together. Try not to overwork the meat, but get it all combined.

3. Form the mixture into balls about the size of a golf ball. You should get about 24 meatballs. Flatten the balls slightly to prevent them from rolling, then arrange them on the sheet pan, about 2 inches apart.

4. Select AIR ROAST, set temperature to 400°F, and set time to 20 minutes. Select START/PAUSE to begin preheating.

5. Once the unit has preheated, slide the pan into the oven.

6. After 10 minutes, remove the pan from the oven and turn over the meatballs. Return the pan to the oven and continue cooking.

7. When cooking is complete, remove the pan from the oven. Place the meatballs on a rack. Wipe off the sheet pan (it doesn't have to be completely clean; you just want to remove the fat from the meatballs. If you can't help yourself, you can wash it.)

8. Open the rolls, cut-side up, on the sheet pan. Place 3 to 4 meatballs on the base of each roll, and top each sandwich with ¼ cup of marinara sauce. Divide the mozzarella among the top halves of the buns and sprinkle the remaining 2 tablespoons of Parmesan cheese over the mozzarella.

9. Select AIR BROIL, set temperature to HIGH, and set time to 4 minutes. Select START/PAUSE to begin preheating.

10. Once the unit has preheated, slide the pan into the oven. Check the sandwiches after 2 minutes; the mozzarella cheese should be melted and bubbling slightly.

11. When cooking is complete, remove the pan from the oven. Close the sandwiches and serve.

Per serving: *Calories: 980; Total Fat: 60g; Saturated Fat: 22g; Cholesterol: 226mg; Sodium: 1632mg; Carbohydrates: 56g; Fiber: 3g; Protein: 56g*

Sausage and Mushroom Calzones

SERVES 4

As much as I like pizza, there's something irresistible about its cousin, the calzone. Maybe it's the way you break through the golden crust to discover the filling within; maybe it's that a calzone is portable. Maybe I just like extra crust.

FAMILY FAVORITE

PREP TIME: 10 minutes
AIR ROAST: 24 minutes
TOTAL TIME: 35 minutes

HACK IT: To save time, replace the Italian sausage with already cooked meat such as sliced pepperoni or crumbled leftover Scratch Meatball Subs (page 166).

2 links Italian sausages (about ½ pound)

1 pound store-bought pizza dough or frozen bread dough, thawed

3 tablespoons extra-virgin olive oil, divided

¼ cup Marinara Sauce (page 195) or store-bought variety

½ cup Oven-Roasted Mushrooms (page 201)

1 cup shredded mozzarella cheese or mozzarella blend

1. Place the sausages on the sheet pan.

2. Select AIR ROAST, set temperature to 375ºF, and set time to 12 minutes. Select START/PAUSE to begin preheating.

3. Once the unit has preheated, slide the pan into the oven.

4. After 6 minutes, remove the pan from the oven and turn over the sausages. Return the pan to the oven and continue cooking.

5. While the sausages cook, divide the pizza dough into 4 equal pieces. One at a time, place a piece of dough onto a square of parchment paper 9 inches in diameter. Brush the dough on both sides with ¾ teaspoon of olive oil, then top the dough with another piece of parchment. Press the dough into a 7-inch circle. Remove the top piece of parchment and set aside. Repeat with the remaining pieces of dough.

6. When cooking is complete, remove the pan from the oven. Place the sausages on a cutting board. Let them cool for several minutes, then slice into ¼-inch rounds and cut

each round into 4 pieces. (Don't worry if the very center of the sausage isn't cooked; it will cook again inside the calzones.)

7. One at a time, spread a tablespoon of marinara sauce over half of a dough circle, leaving a ½-inch border at the edges. Cover with a quarter of the sausage pieces and add a quarter of the mushrooms. Sprinkle with ¼ cup of cheese. Pull the other side of the dough over the filling and pinch the edges together to seal. Transfer from the parchment to the sheet pan. Repeat with the other rounds of dough, sauce, sausage, mushrooms, and cheese.

8. Brush the tops of the calzones with 1 tablespoon of olive oil.

9. Select AIR ROAST, set temperature to 450°F, and set time to 12 minutes. Select START/PAUSE to begin preheating.

10. Once the unit has preheated, slide the pan into the oven.

11. After 6 minutes, remove the pan from the oven. The calzones should be golden brown. Turn over the calzones and brush the tops with the remaining 1 tablespoon of olive oil. Return the pan to the oven and continue cooking.

12. When cooking is complete, the crust should be a deep golden brown on both sides. Remove the pan from the oven. The center will be molten; let cool for several minutes before serving.

Per serving: *Calories: 602; Total Fat: 37g; Saturated Fat: 12g; Cholesterol: 68mg; Sodium: 849mg; Carbohydrates: 50g; Fiber: 4g; Protein: 24g*

Ravioli with Meat Sauce

SERVES 4

If you've made the meatballs for the Scratch Meatball Subs (page 166), you'll have leftovers, and this is a great way to use them up. If not, you can use store-bought frozen (then thawed) meatballs, cooked Italian sausage, or even just cooked ground beef, if you have some languishing in the fridge.

NUT-FREE,
5-INGREDIENT, UNDER
30 MINUTES

PREP TIME: 10 minutes
BAKE: 10 minutes
TOTAL TIME: 20 minutes

1 (20-ounce) package
  frozen cheese ravioli

1 teaspoon kosher salt or
  ½ teaspoon fine salt

1¼ cups water

6 Scratch Meatballs
  (page 166), crumbled

2½ cups Marinara
  Sauce (page 195) or
  store-bought variety

¼ cup grated Parmesan
  cheese, for garnish

1. Place the ravioli in an even layer on the sheet pan. Stir the salt into the water until dissolved and pour it over the ravioli.

2. Select BAKE, set temperature to 450°F, and set time to 10 minutes. Select START/PAUSE to begin preheating.

3. Once the unit has preheated, slide the pan into the oven.

4. While the ravioli is cooking, mix the crumbled meatballs into the marinara sauce in a medium bowl.

5. After 6 minutes, remove the pan from the oven. Blot off any remaining water, or drain the ravioli and return them to the pan. Pour the meat sauce over the ravioli. Return the pan to the oven and continue cooking.

6. When cooking is complete, remove the pan from the oven. The ravioli should be tender and sauce heated through. Gently stir the ingredients. Serve the ravioli with the Parmesan cheese, if desired.

Per Serving: Calories: 545; Total Fat: 24g; Saturated Fat: 10g; Cholesterol: 123mg; Sodium: 731mg; Carbohydrates: 56g; Fiber: 5g; Protein: 29g

Pork Fried Rice with Mushrooms and Peas

Fried rice is by far the best way to use up leftover rice, which becomes dry and stiff when refrigerated (it's because of a process called starch retrogradation, if you want to impress your friends). But when reheated with a savory sauce and chopped meat and vegetables, it turns into a delightful meal. Easy, too!

DAIRY-FREE, NUT-FREE, UNDER 30 MINUTES

PREP TIME: 10 minutes
AIR ROAST: 12 minutes
TOTAL TIME: 25 minutes

3 scallions, diced (about ½ cup)

½ red bell pepper, diced (about ½ cup)

2 teaspoons sesame oil

½ pound pork tenderloin, diced

½ cup Asian-Style Sauce (page 197)

½ cup frozen peas, thawed

½ cup Oven-Roasted Mushrooms (page 201)

2 cups Oven Rice (page 203)

1 egg, beaten

1. Place the scallions and red pepper on the sheet pan. Drizzle with the sesame oil and toss the vegetables to coat them in the oil.

2. Select AIR ROAST, set temperature to 375ºF, and set time to 12 minutes. Select START/PAUSE to begin preheating.

3. Once the unit has preheated, slide the pan into the oven.

4. While the vegetables are cooking, place the pork in a large bowl. Add the sauce, peas, mushrooms, and rice and toss to coat the ingredients with the sauce.

5. After about 4 minutes, remove the pan from the oven. Place the pork mixture on the pan and stir the scallions and peppers into the pork and rice. Return the pan to the oven and continue cooking.

CONTINUED ▶

6. After another 6 minutes, remove the pan from the oven. Move the rice mixture to the sides to create an empty circle in the middle of the pan. Pour the egg in the circle. Return the pan to the oven and continue cooking.

7. When cooking is complete, remove the pan from the oven and stir the egg to scramble it. Stir the egg into the fried rice mixture. Serve immediately.

Per serving: *Calories: 245; Total Fat: 6g; Saturated Fat: 2g; Cholesterol: 73mg; Sodium: 467mg; Carbohydrates: 32g; Fiber: 2g; Protein: 16g*

Teriyaki Pork and Pineapple Skewers

SERVES 4

As with the Southwestern Chicken Skewers with Corn Salad (page 124), this recipe can be a fun family activity to assemble—that way, everyone gets to personalize their own dinner. What I really love about cooking with pork is that the meat beautifully takes on the flavor of whatever sauce or rub you use.

DAIRY-FREE, NUT-FREE, 5-INGREDIENT, UNDER 30 MINUTES

PREP TIME: 10 minutes
AIR ROAST: 12 minutes
TOTAL TIME: 27 minutes

ACCESSORIES: 12 (9- to 12-inch) wooden skewers soaked in water for about 30 minutes

¼ **teaspoon kosher salt or ⅛ teaspoon fine salt**

1 **medium pork tenderloin (about 1 pound), cut into 1½-inch chunks**

1 **red bell pepper, seeded and cut into 1-inch pieces**

1 **green bell pepper, seeded and cut into 1-inch pieces**

2 **cups fresh pineapple chunks**

¾ **cup Teriyaki Sauce (page 199) or store-bought variety**

1. Sprinkle the salt over the pork cubes.

2. Alternate the pork, bell peppers, and pineapple on the skewers, making about 12 skewers (if you use the larger skewers, you'll probably only need 8). Liberally brush the skewers with about half of the Teriyaki Sauce.

3. Select AIR ROAST, set temperature to 375°F, and set time to 10 minutes. Select START/PAUSE to begin preheating.

4. Once the unit has preheated, slide the pan into the oven.

5. After about 5 minutes, remove the pan from the oven. Turn over the skewers and brush with the remaining teriyaki sauce. Return the pan to the oven and continue cooking.

6. When cooking is complete, the vegetables should be tender and browned in spots, and the pork browned and cooked through. Remove the pan from the oven and serve.

Per serving: Calories: 250; Total Fat: 4g; Saturated Fat: 2g; Cholesterol: 65mg; Sodium: 999mg; Carbohydrates: 31g; Fiber: 2g; Protein: 23g

Prosciutto and Asparagus Tart

SERVES 4 AS A MAIN COURSE; 8 AS AN APPETIZER

This elegant tart makes an impressive first course, or, paired with a salad, a great choice for a special lunch. Make sure to use nice, thick asparagus spears for this dish; thin ones will overcook and become stringy, and no one likes that. It might take more than a pound to fill the tart; use whatever you need.

NUT-FREE, 5-INGREDIENT

PREP TIME: 10 minutes
BAKE: 25 minutes
TOTAL TIME: 35 minutes

SUBSTITUTION: If you don't have a good aged balsamic vinegar, don't worry; just leave it out. The tart is delicious without it. But avoid using an inexpensive, thin vinegar. While those are fine for salad dressing, they're not subtle enough for this tart.

1 sheet (½ package) frozen puff pastry, thawed

All-purpose flour, for dusting

½ cup grated Parmesan cheese

1 pound (or more) asparagus, trimmed

8 ounces thinly sliced prosciutto, sliced into ribbons about ½-inch wide

2 teaspoons aged balsamic vinegar

1. Unwrap and unfold the puff pastry on a lightly floured cutting board. Using a rolling pin, roll it very lightly, just to press the folds together. Place it on the sheet pan.

2. Roll about ½ inch of the pastry edges up to form a ridge around the perimeter. Crimp the corners together so you have a solid rim around the pastry. Prick the bottom of the pastry all over with a fork (this will keep it flat as it bakes). Sprinkle the cheese over the bottom of the pastry.

3. Trim the asparagus spears so they fit within the border of the pastry shell. Arrange them on top of the cheese in a single layer. You can point all the spears the same way, but I think it looks best to alternate, with 4 or 5 spears pointing one way, then the next few pointing the opposite direction. Arrange the prosciutto over the top more or less evenly.

4. Select BAKE, set temperature to 375ºF, and set time to 25 minutes. Select START/PAUSE to begin preheating.

CONTINUED ▶

5. Once the unit has preheated, slide the pan into the oven.

6. After about 15 minutes, check the tart, rotating the pan if the crust is not browning evenly. Continue cooking.

7. When cooking is complete, the pastry should be golden brown, and the edges of the prosciutto pieces browned. Remove the pan from the oven. Let the tart cool for a few minutes before slicing. Just before serving, drizzle the balsamic vinegar over the tart.

Per serving: *Calories: 483; Total Fat: 29g; Saturated Fat: 9g; Cholesterol: 40mg; Sodium: 966mg; Carbohydrates: 33g; Fiber: 3g; Protein: 23g*

Tandoori Lamb Chops

SERVES 4

When I lived in San Francisco, there was an absurdly inexpensive Indian restaurant that delivered. I took advantage of it way too often; I just couldn't resist their tandoori lamb chops. This is my version of that favorite. Of course, I don't have a tandoor*—a clay oven that cooks at about 900°F—but the spices are close, and the result is delicious.*

GLUTEN-FREE, NUT-FREE, UNDER 30 MINUTES

PREP TIME: 10 minutes
AIR ROAST: 10 minutes
AIR BROIL: 10 minutes
TOTAL TIME: 30 minutes

VARIATION: This marinade is also great with boneless chicken thighs.

- 8 (½-inch thick) lamb loin chops (about 2 pounds)
- 2 teaspoons kosher salt or 1 teaspoon fine salt, divided
- ¾ cup plain whole milk yogurt
- 1 tablespoon freshly grated ginger (1- or 2-inch piece) or 1 teaspoon ground ginger
- 2 garlic cloves, minced or smashed
- 1 teaspoon smoked paprika
- ½ teaspoon cayenne pepper
- 1 teaspoon curry powder
- 12 ounces small red potatoes, quartered
- Cooking oil spray

1. Salt the lamb chops on both sides with 1 teaspoon of kosher salt and let sit while you prepare the marinade.

2. In a large bowl, whisk together the yogurt, ginger, garlic, paprika, cayenne pepper, curry powder, and remaining 1 teaspoon of kosher salt. Pour all but 2 tablespoons of the marinade into a resealable plastic bag, leaving those 2 tablespoons in the bowl. Place the lamb chops in the bag. Squeeze out as much air as possible and squish the bag around to coat the chops with the marinade. Set aside.

3. Add the potatoes to the bowl with the remaining marinade and toss to coat. Spray the sheet pan with cooking oil spray. Place the potatoes on the pan.

CONTINUED ▸

4. Select AIR ROAST, set temperature to 375ºF, and set time to 10 minutes. Select START/PAUSE to begin preheating.

5. Once the unit has preheated, slide the pan into the oven.

6. When cooking is complete, remove the pan from the oven. Remove the chops from the marinade, draining off all but a thin coat (and discarding the marinade and plastic bag), and place them on the sheet pan.

7. Select AIR BROIL, set temperature to HIGH, and set time to 10 minutes. Select START/PAUSE to begin preheating.

8. Once the unit has preheated, slide the pan into the oven. After 5 minutes, remove the pan from the oven and turn over the chops and potatoes. Return the pan to the oven and continue cooking.

9. When cooking is complete, the lamb should read 145ºF for medium rare on a meat thermometer; continue cooking for an additional few minutes if you want it more well done. Remove the pan from the oven and serve.

Per serving: *Calories: 575; Total Fat: 41g; Saturated Fat: 18g; Cholesterol: 126mg; Sodium: 341mg; Carbohydrates: 17g; Fiber: 2g; Protein: 32g*

Lemon Shortbread, *page 188*

9

Desserts and Staples

Peach and Blueberry Galette

Whether you call it a galette or a crostata, this free-form open fruit pie is sure to be a winner. Starting with a refrigerated piecrust from the grocery store makes it easy and fast, but feel free to substitute your favorite sturdy piecrust recipe, if that's the way you roll. Use whatever fruit is in season, and you'll have an elegant dessert for company in the blink of an eye.

NUT-FREE, VEGETARIAN, 30 MINUTES

PREP TIME: 10 minutes
BAKE: 20 minutes
TOTAL TIME: 30 minutes

2 large peaches or nectarines, peeled and cut into ½-inch slices (about 2 cups)

1 pint blueberries, rinsed and picked through (about 2 cups)

⅓ cup plus 2 tablespoons granulated sugar, divided

2 tablespoons unbleached all-purpose flour

¼ teaspoon ground allspice or cinnamon

½ teaspoon grated lemon zest (optional)

Pinch kosher or fine salt

1 (9-inch) refrigerated piecrust (or use homemade)

2 teaspoons unsalted butter, cut into pea-size pieces

1 large egg, beaten

1. In a medium bowl, gently mix the peaches and blueberries with ⅓ cup of sugar, flour, allspice, lemon zest (if using), and salt.

2. On the sheet pan, unroll the crust, patching any tears if necessary. Arrange the fruit in the center of the crust, leaving about 1½ inches of space around the edges. Distribute the butter pieces over the fruit. Fold the outside edge of the crust over the outer circle of the fruit, making pleats as necessary. Brush the crust with the egg. Sprinkle the remaining 2 tablespoons of sugar over the crust and fruit.

3. Select BAKE, set temperature to 350°F, and set time to 20 minutes. Select START/PAUSE to begin preheating.

CONTINUED ▶

4. Once the unit has preheated, slide the pan into the oven.

5. After about 15 minutes, check the galette, rotating the pan if the crust is not browning evenly. The galette is done when the crust is deep golden brown and the fruit is bubbling.

6. Remove the pan from the oven and let cool for 10 minutes, then cut into wedges and serve warm.

Per serving: Calories: 261; Total Fat: 9g; Saturated Fat: 3g; Cholesterol: 34mg; Sodium: 148mg; Carbohydrates: 44g; Fiber: 3g; Protein: 3g

Oatmeal Chocolate Chip Cookie Bars

MAKES 4 DOZEN (1-BY-1½-INCH) BARS

My least favorite part of making cookies is portioning out the dough and baking sheet after sheet of them. Depending on the batch size, it seems to take forever. That's the advantage to baking bars instead of individual cookies, and with the Ninja® Foodi™ Digital Air Fry Oven, you can make a giant batch all at once. This recipe combines chocolate chips and oatmeal for two favorites in one bar.

NUT-FREE, FAMILY FAVORITE, VEGETARIAN, UNDER 30 MINUTES

PREP TIME: 10 minutes
BAKE: 20 minutes
TOTAL TIME: 30 minutes

DID YOU KNOW: There's no official definition of semisweet or bittersweet chocolate, and that's one of the reasons many chocolate makers now include a percentage on their packaging. If you see 60% or 72% cacao on your chocolate chips or bar, it means that 60 or 72 percent of that chocolate is cocoa liquid or solids—the rest being primarily sugar or, in the case of milk chocolate, milk solids. So the higher the number, the darker and less sweet the chocolate is. For these bars, I like chocolate chips that are around 60 percent.

1 cup unsalted butter, at room temperature
1 cup dark brown sugar
½ cup granulated sugar
2 large eggs
1 tablespoon vanilla extract
Pinch salt

1½ cups all-purpose flour
1 teaspoon baking soda
1 teaspoon baking powder
2 cups old-fashioned rolled oats
2 cups chocolate chips

1. In a large mixing bowl or stand mixer, beat together the butter, brown sugar, and granulated sugar until creamy and light in color.

2. Add the eggs one at a time, mixing after each addition. Add the vanilla and salt and mix to combine.

3. In a separate bowl, combine the flour, baking soda, baking powder, and oats. Add to the butter mixture and mix until combined. By hand, stir in the chocolate chips. (If you have a stand mixer, you can do this with the machine, but hand mixers usually aren't strong enough to handle these ingredients.)

4. Spread the dough onto the sheet pan in an even layer. It will fill the entire pan.

5. Select BAKE, set temperature to 350°F, and set time to 20 minutes. Select START/PAUSE to begin preheating.

CONTINUED ▶

6. Once the unit has preheated, slide the pan into the oven.

7. After 15 minutes, check the cookie, rotating the pan if the crust is not browning evenly. Continue cooking for a total of 18 to 20 minutes or until golden brown. Remove the pan from the oven and let cool completely before cutting.

Per serving (1 bar): Calories: 123; Total Fat: 6g; Saturated Fat: 4g; Cholesterol: 20mg; Sodium: 41mg; Carbohydrates: 15g; Fiber: 1g; Protein: 2g

Lemon Shortbread

Like the Oatmeal Chocolate Chip Cookie Bars (page 185), these cookies are a great choice when you need dessert for a crowd. Whether you're going to a bake sale or a potluck, you'll be a star when you show up with these crisp, buttery bars with their hint of lemon.

NUT-FREE, 5-INGREDIENT, VEGETARIAN

PREP TIME: 10 minutes
BAKE: 36 to 40 minutes
TOTAL TIME: 50 minutes

VARIATION: For a change, omit the lemon zest and stir in ½ cup very finely diced crystalized ginger. Plain shortbread is also fabulous.

1 cup granulated sugar

1 tablespoon grated lemon zest

1 pound unsalted butter, at room temperature

¼ teaspoon fine salt

4 cups all-purpose flour

⅓ cup cornstarch

Cooking oil spray

1. In a stand mixer fitted with the paddle attachment, beat the sugar and lemon zest on medium speed for a minute or two, then let sit for about 5 minutes. (If you don't have a stand mixer, use a hand mixer.) Add the butter and salt, and beat until well blended and fluffy.

2. In a large bowl, whisk together the flour and cornstarch. Gradually add the dry ingredients to the butter mixture and mix just until combined. (If you're using a hand mixer, you may have to finish mixing by hand; the dough is quite stiff.)

3. Spray the sheet pan with cooking oil spray and fit in a piece of parchment paper. Press the dough into the pan until very even and smooth.

4. Select BAKE, set temperature to 325°F, and set time to 36 minutes. Select START/PAUSE to begin preheating.

5. Once the unit has preheated, slide the pan into the oven.

6. After 20 minutes, check the shortbread, rotating the pan if it is not browning evenly. Continue for 16 minutes more, or until light golden brown. This will yield shortbread bars that are crumbly and just slightly soft. For crisper shortbread, cook for an additional 3 to 4 minutes, then turn the oven off and let the shortbread stay in the oven for a few more minutes until it's a few shades darker.

7. When cooking is complete, remove the pan from the oven. These bars are easiest to cut when they're slightly warm. Let cool. If you like, dust the bars with confectioners' sugar or granulated sugar.

Per serving (1 cookie): *Calories: 125; Total Fat: 8g; Saturated Fat: 5g; Cholesterol: 20mg; Sodium: 13mg; Carbohydrates: 13g; Fiber: 0g; Protein: 1g*

Caramel Pear Tart

SERVES 8

The trick to a crisp bottom crust with this delicious, easy tart is to coat the puff pastry with caramel before adding the sliced pears. Otherwise, the liquid from the fruit as it cooks will result in a soggy mess. The pears will give off some liquid (slightly underripe pears are actually preferable since they give off a bit less), but it combines with the caramel syrup to produce a great sauce for the fruit.

NUT-FREE, 5-INGREDIENT, VEGETARIAN

PREP TIME: 15 minutes
BAKE: 25 minutes
TOTAL TIME: 40 minutes

Juice of 1 lemon

3 medium or 2 large ripe or almost ripe pears (preferably Bosc or Anjou)

1 sheet (½ package) frozen puff pastry, thawed

All-purpose flour, for dusting

4 tablespoons caramel sauce (I use Smuckers Salted Caramel), divided

1. In a large bowl, mix the lemon juice with about 1 quart of water.

2. Peel the pears and remove the stems. Cut them in half through the stem end. Use a melon baller to remove the seeds and cut out the blossom end. Remove any tough fibers between the stem end and the center. As you work, place the pear halves in the acidulated water.

3. Unwrap and unfold the puff pastry on a lightly floured cutting board. Using a rolling pin, roll it very lightly, just to press the folds together. Transfer it to the sheet pan.

4. Roll about ½ inch of the pastry edges up to form a ridge around the perimeter. Crimp the corners together so you have a solid rim around the pastry to hold in the liquid as the tart cooks. Brush the bottom of the pastry with 2 tablespoons of caramel sauce. (If the sauce is cold, it may be very stiff. You can microwave it for a few seconds, or set the jar in a bowl of very hot water for a few minutes to make it easier to brush).

CONTINUED ▶

5. Remove the pear halves from the water and blot them dry with paper towels. Place one of the halves on the board cut-side down and cut ¼-inch-thick slices radially (think of cutting really thin wedges, rather than slicing straight up and down). Repeat with the remaining halves. Arrange the pear slices over the pastry. You can get as fancy as you like, but I find that three rows of slices fills the tart, looks good, and isn't difficult to achieve. Drizzle the remaining 2 tablespoons of caramel sauce over the pears.

6. Select BAKE, set temperature to 350°F, and set time to 25 minutes. Select START/PAUSE to begin preheating.

7. Once the unit has preheated, slide the pan into the oven.

8. After 15 minutes, check the tart, rotating the pan if the crust is not browning evenly. Continue cooking.

9. When cooking is complete, the pastry will be golden brown, the pears soft, and the caramel bubbling. Remove the pan from the oven and let the tart cool for about 10 minutes. The tart can be served warm or at room temperature. If there is a lot of liquid floating around the pears, you can blot it off with paper towels, which will keep the crust crisper and won't diminish the flavor.

Per serving: *Calories: 227; Total Fat: 12g; Saturated Fat: 3g; Cholesterol: 0mg; Sodium: 112mg; Carbohydrates: 30g; Fiber: 3g; Protein: 3g*

Quick Baklava

I love traditional baklava. I made it once, in a cooking class, years ago. It's not that difficult if you're used to working with phyllo dough, but it takes forever. You think you're done when it's baked, but then there's a whole soaking-the-pastry-with-syrup step, which is just cruel when all you want is to start eating it. This version starts with frozen phyllo shells, and substitutes a little honey, straight from the squeezy bear, in place of the syrup. Not traditional, but delicious, and it's ready to eat in less than an hour.

VEGETARIAN, UNDER 30 MINUTES

PREP TIME: 10 minutes
AIR FRY: 4 minutes
BAKE: 12 minutes
TOTAL TIME: 26 minutes

ACCESSORIES:
Air Fry Basket

SUBSTITUTION: While walnuts and pistachios are traditional in baklava, you can use all walnuts if you can't find shelled pistachios. You can even use pecans or almonds if you have them on hand. Avoid peanuts; their flavor is too assertive for this dessert.

1 cup shelled raw pistachios

1 cup walnut pieces

½ cup unsalted butter, melted

3 tablespoons granulated sugar

¼ cup plus 2 tablespoons honey, divided

1 teaspoon ground cinnamon

2 (1.9-ounce) packages frozen miniature phyllo tart shells

1. Place the pistachios and walnuts in the Air Fry basket in an even layer.

2. Select AIR FRY, set temperature to 350°F, and set time to 4 minutes. Select START/PAUSE to begin preheating.

3. Once the unit has preheated, slide the basket and sheet pan into the oven.

4. After 2 minutes, remove the basket and stir the nuts. Return the basket to the oven and continue cooking until the nuts are golden brown and fragrant, 1 to 2 minutes more.

5. While the nuts are toasting, place the butter into a medium bowl. Add the sugar, ¼ cup of honey, and cinnamon. Stir to combine.

CONTINUED ▶

6. When the nuts are toasted, remove the basket and pan from the oven and place them on a cutting board and let cool for a couple of minutes. Finely chop the nuts—not so that they're pulverized, but so no large chunks remain. If you have a food processor, a few pulses of the blade should do it. If you have an old-fashioned nut chopper, this is a great time to pull it out. Add the chopped nuts, with all the "nut dust," to the sugar mixture and stir to combine.

7. Place the phyllo cups on the sheet pan, which will be cool by now. Evenly fill the phyllo cups with the nut mixture, mounding it up. (You'll think you have too much filling, but you won't; trust me.) As you work, stir the nuts in the bowl frequently so that the syrup is even distributed throughout the filling.

8. Select BAKE, set temperature to 350°F, and set time to 12 minutes. Select START/PAUSE to begin preheating.

9. Once the unit has preheated, slide the pan into the oven. After about 8 minutes, check the cups, and rotate the pan if the they are not browning evenly. Continue cooking until the cups are dark golden brown and the syrup is bubbling (it might ooze out; don't worry about that).

10. As soon as you remove the baklava from the oven, drizzle each cup with about ⅛ teaspoon or so of the remaining honey over the top. Let cool completely before serving.

Per serving (3 baklava cups): *Calories: 312; Total Fat: 23g; Saturated Fat: 7g; Cholesterol: 24mg; Sodium: 100mg; Carbohydrates: 25g; Fiber: 2g; Protein: 5g*

Marinara Sauce

This is the only recipe in the book that requires the stovetop and a saucepan, but it's a good one to have in your repertoire. I use it in several recipes throughout the book, and while you can certainly buy commercial marinara sauce for them, it's not difficult and certainly less expensive to make your own. You can refrigerate it for several days, or freeze for up to a month.

DAIRY-FREE, GLUTEN-FREE, NUT-FREE, VEGAN

PREP TIME: 15 minutes
COOK TIME: 30 minutes
TOTAL TIME: 45 minutes

¼ cup extra-virgin olive oil

1 small onion, chopped (about ½ cup)

3 garlic cloves, minced

2 tablespoons minced or puréed sun-dried tomatoes (optional)

1 (28-ounce) can crushed tomatoes

½ teaspoon dried oregano

½ teaspoon dried basil

¼ teaspoon red pepper flakes

1 teaspoon kosher salt or ½ teaspoon fine salt

1. Place the oil into a medium saucepan over medium heat. When the oil shimmers, add the onion and garlic. Cook, stirring frequently, for 2 to 3 minutes, or until the onion has started to soften. Add the sun-dried tomatoes (if using) and cook for 1 minute, or until fragrant. Add the crushed tomatoes and stir to combine, scraping the bottom of the pot if there is anything stuck. Stir in the oregano, basil, red pepper flakes, and salt.

2. Bring to a simmer and cover the saucepan. Cook, stirring occasionally, for about 30 minutes.

3. Turn off the heat and let the sauce cool for about 10 minutes. Taste and adjust the seasoning, adding more salt if necessary. Refrigerate in an airtight container for up to a week or freeze for 4 to 6 weeks if not using right away.

Per serving (½ cup): *Calories: 133; Total Fat: 8g; Saturated Fat: 1g; Cholesterol: 0mg; Sodium: 353mg; Carbohydrates: 12g; Fiber: 5g; Protein: 3g*

Red Enchilada Sauce, Caesar Dressing, Teriyaki Sauce, and Southwestern Seasoning, *pages 198–200, 206*

Asian-Style Sauce

I use some variation of this sauce in many Asian-inspired dishes, from stir-fries to roasted pork. I don't claim it's authentic, but it's tasty and it goes together quickly. Don't worry that all your Asian-inspired dishes will taste the same; a few additions can change the character of every dish you use it in. This sauce will last for three days in the refrigerator if you want to make it ahead.

DAIRY-FREE, NUT-FREE, VEGETARIAN OPTION, UNDER 30 MINUTES

PREP TIME: 15 minutes

HACK IT: If you can find Dorot Brand frozen garlic and ginger cubes, they're a great product and a big time-saver.

¼ cup low-sodium chicken or vegetable stock

¼ cup rice vinegar

¼ cup hoisin sauce

3 tablespoons soy sauce

1 teaspoon chili-garlic sauce or sriracha (or more to taste)

1 tablespoon minced or pressed garlic

1 tablespoon minced or grated ginger

In a small bowl, whisk together all the ingredients or place in a jar with a tight-fitting lid and shake to combine.

Per serving (¼ cup): Calories: 59; Total Fat: 1g; Saturated Fat: 0g; Cholesterol: 0mg; Sodium: 897mg; Carbohydrates: 10g; Fiber: 1g; Protein: 1g

Red Enchilada Sauce

If you want really great enchiladas, try making your own sauce. You'll need a blender and access to ancho chiles. If you can find the chiles, it's not hard to make. This will make plenty for a batch of Cheese and Mushroom Enchiladas with Spicy Beans and Corn (page 72). But make a double batch; it freezes beautifully in an airtight container for up to a month.

DAIRY-FREE, GLUTEN-FREE, NUT-FREE, VEGAN, UNDER 30 MINUTES

PREP TIME: 15 minutes

3 large ancho chiles, stems and seeds removed, torn into pieces

1½ cups very hot water

2 garlic cloves, peeled and lightly smashed

2 teaspoons kosher salt or 1 teaspoon fine salt

½ teaspoon dried oregano

½ teaspoon ground cumin

1½ teaspoons sugar

2 tablespoons wine vinegar

1. Place the chile pieces in the hot water and let sit for 10 to 15 minutes.

2. Pour the chiles and water into a blender jar and add the garlic, salt, oregano, cumin, sugar, and vinegar. Blend until smooth.

Per serving (2 cups): *Calories: 31; Total Fat: 0g; Saturated Fat: 0g; Cholesterol: 0mg; Sodium: 105mg; Carbohydrates: 7g; Fiber: 0g; Protein: 1g*

Teriyaki Sauce

If you've never had homemade teriyaki sauce, you'll be surprised how easy—and good—it is. It's best used right after you make it, but it will keep for a couple of days in an airtight container in the refrigerator.

DAIRY-FREE, NUT-FREE, VEGETARIAN, UNDER 30 MINUTES

PREP TIME: 5 minutes

½ cup soy sauce

3 tablespoons honey

1 tablespoon rice vinegar

1 tablespoon rice wine or dry sherry

2 teaspoons minced fresh ginger

2 garlic cloves, smashed

In a small bowl, whisk together all the ingredients.

Per serving (2 tablespoons): Calories: 52; Total Fat: 0g; Saturated Fat: 0g; Cholesterol: 0mg; Sodium: 1220mg; Carbohydrates: 12g; Fiber: 0g; Protein: 1g

Caesar Dressing

If you have an immersion blender, it's quick and easy to make your own Caesar dressing. Don't worry that the anchovy paste will make the dressing taste fishy; the small amount just intensifies the umami flavors of the dressing.

DAIRY-FREE, GLUTEN-
FREE, NUT-FREE,
5-INGREDIENT, UNDER
30 MINUTES

PREP TIME: 5 minutes

1 teaspoon anchovy paste

¼ teaspoon minced
or pressed garlic

¼ teaspoon kosher salt or
⅛ teaspoon fine salt

1 egg

2 tablespoons freshly
squeezed lemon juice

½ cup extra-virgin olive oil

Place all the ingredients in the order listed in a tall narrow container. Place the blade of the immersion blender in the bottom of the container. Turn the blender on and slowly bring it up to the top of the ingredients, repeating if necessary to thoroughly emulsify the dressing.

Per serving (2 tablespoon): Calories: 158; Total Fat: 19g; Saturated Fat: 3g; Cholesterol: 30mg; Sodium: 160mg; Carbohydrates: 0g; Fiber: 0g; Protein: 1g

Oven-Roasted Mushrooms

You may have heard that the only way to cook mushrooms is to add them to a very hot pan on the stove, uncovered, so their water evaporates and they brown instead of steam. Not only is that not the only way to cook them, it's not even the best way. If you steam them in a little water, it allows them to cook while they exude their liquid. Then, after they're cooked, let that liquid evaporate, and they'll brown beautifully in the oil that's left on the sheet pan. You'll never go back.

NUT-FREE, GLUTEN-FREE, DAIRY-FREE OPTION, VEGAN OPTION, 5-INGREDIENT

PREP TIME: 8 minutes
AIR ROAST: 30 minutes
TOTAL TIME: 38 minutes

1 pound button or cremini mushrooms, washed, stems trimmed

¼ cup water

1 teaspoon kosher salt or ½ teaspoon fine salt

3 tablespoons unsalted butter, cut into pieces, or extra-virgin olive oil

1. Place a large piece of aluminum foil on the sheet pan. Cut the mushrooms into quarters or thick slices and place them in the middle of the foil. Spread them out into a single layer as much as possible. Pour the water over them, then sprinkle with the salt and add the butter. Seal the foil, fully enclosing the mushrooms.

2. Select AIR ROAST, set temperature to 325°F, and set time to 15 minutes. Select START/PAUSE to begin preheating.

3. Once the unit has preheated, slide the pan into the oven.

4. After 15 minutes, remove the pan from the oven. Carefully place the foil packet on a cutting board and open it up. Pour the mushrooms and liquid from the foil onto the sheet pan.

5. Select AIR ROAST, set temperature to 350°F, and set time to 15 minutes. Slide the pan into the oven. Select START/PAUSE to begin.

CONTINUED ▶

Oven-Roasted Mushrooms continued

6. After about 10 minutes, remove the pan from the oven and stir the mushrooms. The liquid should be evaporating. Return the pan to the oven and continue cooking.

7. When cooking is complete, the liquid will be mostly gone and the mushrooms will have begun to brown, anywhere from 5 to 15 more minutes. Use immediately or refrigerate in an airtight container up to 5 days.

Per serving (½ cup): *Calories: 132; Total Fat: 11g; Saturated Fat: 7g; Cholesterol: 30mg; Sodium: 205mg; Carbohydrates: 5g; Fiber: 2g; Protein: 5g*

Oven Rice

Rinsing the rice first and then coating it in butter or olive oil ensures that it doesn't stick, and the slow, even heat of the Ninja® Foodi™ Digital Air Fry Oven means no scorching. You can make it ahead, then use it in Pork Fried Rice with Mushrooms and Peas (page 171), Stuffed Rainbow Peppers (page 77), Teriyaki Salmon with Baby Bok Choy (page 108), or Beef and Crispy Broccoli (page 157).

NUT-FREE, GLUTEN-FREE, VEGAN OPTION, 5-INGREDIENT

PREP TIME: 3 minutes
BAKE: 35 minutes
TOTAL TIME: 40 minutes

ACCESSORIES: 8- to 9-inch square or round nonstick baking pan

1 cup long-grain white rice

1 tablespoon unsalted butter, melted, or 1 tablespoon extra-virgin olive oil

2 cups water

1 teaspoon kosher salt or ½ teaspoon fine salt

1. Rinse the rice well under cold water and let drain.

2. Place the butter in the baking pan and add the rice. Stir it to coat with the fat, then pour in the water and add the salt. Stir to dissolve the salt.

3. Select BAKE, set temperature to 325ºF, and set time to 35 minutes. Select START/PAUSE to begin preheating.

4. Once the unit has preheated, slide the pan into the oven.

5. After 20 minutes, remove the pan from the oven and stir the rice. Return the pan to the oven and continue cooking. After 10 more minutes, check the rice again. It should be mostly cooked through, and the water should be absorbed. If not, continue cooking for a few more minutes.

6. When cooking is complete, remove the pan from the oven and cover with aluminum foil. Let sit for 10 minutes, then gently fluff the rice with a fork. Serve immediately, or let cool for 20 minutes, then refrigerate in an airtight container.

Per serving (½ cup): Calories: 97; Total Fat: 2g; Saturated Fat: 1g; Cholesterol: 4mg; Sodium: 292mg; Carbohydrates: 19g; Fiber: 0g; Protein: 2g

Oven Polenta (Grits)

MAKES ABOUT 4 CUPS

This is a recipe to make on the weekend—you can use some the night you make it, and save the rest for meals throughout the week. Yes, you can buy premade polenta at the grocery store. It's fine, if you haven't had homemade. This is better. Yes, it takes a while, but the Ninja® Foodi™ Digital Air Fry Oven does most of the work.

NUT-FREE, GLUTEN-FREE, VEGETARIAN OPTION, 5-INGREDIENT

PREP TIME: 3 minutes
BAKE: 65 minutes
TOTAL TIME: 68 minutes

ACCESSORIES: 8- to 9-inch square or round nonstick baking pan

VARIATION: If you like, stir in ½ cup grated or shredded Parmesan or sharp cheddar cheese when the polenta is done.

1 cup polenta or grits (not instant or quick cook)

2 cups milk

2 cups chicken or vegetable stock

1 teaspoon kosher salt or ½ teaspoon fine salt

2 tablespoons unsalted butter, cut into 4 pieces

1. Place the grits in the baking pan. Add the milk, stock, salt, and butter and stir gently.

2. Select BAKE, set temperature to 325°F, and set time to 1 hour, 5 minutes. Select START/PAUSE to begin preheating.

3. Once the unit has preheated, slide the pan into the oven.

4. After 15 minutes, remove the pan from the oven and stir the polenta. Return the pan to the oven and continue cooking.

5. After 30 minutes, remove the pan again and stir the polenta. Return the pan to the oven and continue cooking. After another 15 minutes (1 hour total), remove the pan from the oven. The polenta should be soft and creamy, with all the liquid absorbed. If necessary, continue cooking for 5 to 10 minutes more.

6. When cooking is complete, remove the pan from the oven. Serve, or let cool to room temperature, then cover and refrigerate for up to 3 days.

Per serving (1 cup): Calories: 141; Total Fat: 8g; Saturated Fat: 5g; Cholesterol: 25mg; Sodium: 318mg; Carbohydrates: 12g; Fiber: 0g; Protein: 5g

DID YOU KNOW: What's the difference, you may ask, between polenta and grits? It depends on who's doing the telling. Some people say that grits have to be made from hominy, which is corn treated with lye to soften it. That may have been true in the past, but not so much anymore. Some people say it's the type of corn that's used, and others say it's the way it's ground. Here's what I know: the usual brand of grits we use, Bob's Red Mill, says—on the label—Grits (aka Polenta). I go with that.

Southwestern Seasoning

Based loosely on a recipe from the Chevys and Rio Bravo Fresh Mex Cookbook, *this is my favorite seasoning blend to use with fajitas and other Southwestern or Mexican-inspired dishes. The cayenne gives it a bit of heat; if you prefer a milder blend, cut the cayenne in half.*

DAIRY-FREE, GLUTEN-FREE, NUT-FREE, UNDER 30 MINUTES

PREP TIME: 5 minutes

3 tablespoons paprika

3 tablespoons ancho chile powder

2 teaspoons cayenne

2 tablespoons freshly ground black pepper

2 teaspoons cumin

1 tablespoon granulated garlic

1 tablespoon granulated onion

2 tablespoons dried oregano

Place all the ingredients in a small bowl and whisk to combine. Store in an airtight container in the pantry.

Per serving (1 tablespoon): *Calories: 21; Total Fat: 1g; Saturated Fat: 0g; Cholesterol: 0mg; Sodium: 21mg; Carbohydrates: 4g; Fiber: 2g; Protein: 1g*

Shawarma Seasoning

While there are several commercial shawarma spice mixtures available, I like to make my own. It does take a fairly well-stocked spice shelf, but nothing in it is too exotic. You can double or triple the recipe and keep the extra in an airtight container for up to a month.

DAIRY-FREE, GLUTEN-FREE, NUT-FREE, UNDER 30 MINUTES

PREP TIME: 5 minutes

1 teaspoon cumin

1 teaspoon smoked paprika

¼ teaspoon kosher salt or ⅛ teaspoon fine salt

¼ teaspoon turmeric

¼ teaspoon allspice

¼ teaspoon cinnamon

¼ teaspoon freshly ground black pepper

¼ teaspoon red pepper flakes

In a small bowl, combine all the ingredients. Store in an airtight container in the pantry.

Per serving (1 teaspoon): *Calories: 7; Total Fat: 0g; Saturated Fat: 0g; Cholesterol: 0mg; Sodium: 196mg; Carbohydrates: 1g; Fiber: 1g; Protein: 0g*

Spicy Pork Lettuce Cups, *page 161*

Ninja® Foodi™ Digital Air Fry Oven
MEAL PLAN AND SHOPPING LIST

To take full advantage of your Ninja Foodi Digital Air Fry Oven, use it to cook every meal! You can also download this meal plan and shopping list from www.callistomediabooks.com/NinjaFoodiDigitalAirFryOven.

MEAL PLAN

Sunday

Breakfast: French Toast Casserole 36
Lunch: Spicy Thai Vegetables 85
Dinner: Sweet-and-Sour Chicken with Oven Rice 136 and 203
Dessert: Quick Baklava 193

Monday

Breakfast: Classic Corned Beef Hash and Eggs 31
Lunch: Roasted Nicoise Salad 101
Snack: Sweet and Spicy Nuts 51
Dinner: Braised Pork Chops with Squash and Apples 164

Tuesday

Breakfast: Artichoke-Mushroom Frittata 38
Lunch: Pork Fried Rice with Mushrooms and Peas 171
Snack: Garlic-Parmesan Crunchy Snack Mix 64
Dinner: Tilapia Meunière with Green Beans and Potatoes 113

Wednesday

Breakfast: Spiced Apple Turnovers 29
Lunch: Scratch Meatball Subs 166
Dinner: Curried Chicken and Sweet Potatoes 139
Dessert: Oatmeal Chocolate Chip Cookie Bars 185

Thursday

Breakfast: Blueberry Sheet Pan Cake 27
Lunch: Warm Caesar Salad with Shrimp 104

Snack: Pepperoni Pizza Bites 58
Dinner: Sweet-and-Spicy Drumsticks with Garlic Green Beans 133

Friday

Breakfast: Mini Cinnamon Sticky Rolls 33
Lunch: Turkey Burgers with Cheddar and Roasted Onions 147
Dinner: Teriyaki Pork and Pineapple Skewers 173
Dessert: Lemon Shortbread 188

Saturday

Breakfast: Eggs Florentine 25
Lunch: Crispy Bean and Cheese Tacos 83
Dinner: Ravioli with Meat Sauce 170
Dessert: Peach and Blueberry Galette 183

SHOPPING LIST

Canned and Bottled Items

- Anchovy paste (1 teaspoon)
- Artichoke hearts (1 cup)
- Black beans, 1 (15-ounce) can
- Chili-garlic sauce (1 teaspoon)
- Hoison sauce (¼ cup)
- Honey (¾ cup plus 1 tablespoon)
- Ketchup (2 tablespoons)
- Maple syrup (1 tablespoon)
- Mayonnaise (⅓ cup)
- Mustard, Dijon (¼ cup)
- Oil, olive, extra-virgin
- Oil, sesame (2 tablespoons)
- Oil, vegetable (½ cup)
- Olives, Nicoise (⅓ cup)
- Rice wine (1 tablespoon)
- Salsa (½ cup)
- Soy sauce (¾ cup plus 1 tablespoon)
- Stock, chicken, low-sodium (¾ cup)
- Sun-dried tomatoes (2 tablespoons)
- Thai curry paste, red or green (2 teaspoons)
- Thai sweet chili sauce (⅓ cup)
- Tomatoes, crushed, 1 (28-ounce) can
- Tuna, oil-packed, 2 (5-ounce) cans
- Vinegar, red (3 tablespoons)
- Vinegar, rice (½ cup)
- Water chestnuts (1 can)
- Worcestershire sauce (2 teaspoons)

Dairy and Eggs

- Butter, unsalted (11 sticks)
- Cheese, cheddar, sharp, slices (¼ pound)
- Cheese, Monterey Jack, grated (¼ pound)
- Cheese, mozzarella, shredded (2½ cups)
- Cheese, Parmesan, grated (1 cup)
- Cheese, ricotta (¼ pound)
- Cream, heavy (2 tablespoons)
- Crescent rolls 1 (8-ounce) can
- Eggs (2 dozen)
- Milk, whole (3 cups)

Frozen Foods

- Mango slices (1 cup)
- Peas (½ cup)
- Phyllo tart shells, 2 (1.9-ounce) packages
- Piecrust, 1 (9-inch)
- Puff Pastry (1 package)
- Spinach (3 cups)

Meat

- Chicken breasts, boneless, skinless (1½ pounds)
- Chicken drumsticks (8)
- Chicken thighs, boneless, skinless (1 pound)
- Corned beef (¾ pound)
- Ground chuck (1 pound)
- Italian sausage (1 pound)
- Pepperoni (2 ounces)
- Pork loin chops, boneless (4)
- Pork tenderloin (2½ pounds)
- Shrimp, medium (1 pound)
- Tilapia fillets, 4 (8-ounce)
- Turkey, ground (1¼ pounds)

Pantry Items

- Allspice (⅜ teaspoon)
- Almonds, toasted (½ cup)
- Baguette (1)
- Baking powder (1 teaspoon)
- Baking soda (1 teaspoon)
- Basil (½ teaspoon)
- Bisquick (1½ cups)
- Black pepper
- Bread crumbs, panko (½ cup)
- Bread, slices (4)

- Cayenne pepper (1 teaspoon)
- Cereal, Chex-style (2 cups)
- Chili powder (1½ teaspoons)
- Chocolate chips (2 cups)
- Cinnamon (3½ teaspoons)
- Cooking oil spray
- Cornstarch (½ cup)
- Crackers, oyster (2 cups)
- Curry powder (1 tablespoon)
- Flour, all-purpose (5½ cups)
- Garlic, granulated (1¾ teaspoons)
- Hamburger buns (4)
- Hoagie or sub rolls (4)
- Oats, old-fashioned rolled (2 cups)
- Oregano (½ teaspoon)
- Peanuts (½ cup)
- Pistachios, raw, shelled (1 cup)
- Red pepper flakes (¼ teaspoon)
- Rice, long-grain white (1 cup)
- Salt, fine
- Salt, kosher
- Saltines (24)
- Sesame sticks (1 cup)
- Sugar, brown (2 cup)
- Sugar, confectioners' (2 tablespoons)
- Sugar, white (3 cups)
- Thyme (1 teaspoon)
- Tortillas, corn (8)
- Tortillas, flour, 8 (6-inch)
- Vanilla extract (2 tablespoons)
- Walnut halves (1 pound)
- Walnut pieces (1 cup)

Produce

- Apple, Gala or Braeburn (2)
- Bell pepper, green (1)
- Bell pepper, red (5)
- Blueberries (2 pints)
- Brussels sprouts (¾ pound)
- Butternut squash (1 pound)
- Cabbage, Napa (1 head)
- Carrot (1)
- Chile, ancho (3)
- Chile, serrano (1)
- Cilantro (¼ cup)
- Garlic cloves (12)
- Ginger (1 medium knob)
- Green beans (2 pounds)
- Jalapeño (1)
- Lemons (3)
- Lettuce, butter (1 head)
- Lettuce, romaine (3 heads)
- Limes (1)
- Mushrooms, button or cremini (1 pound)
- Onion (6)
- Parsley (2 tablespoons)
- Peaches (2)
- Pineapple (1)
- Potatoes, sweet (2)
- Potatoes, red (10 ounces)
- Potatoes, Yukon Gold (1½ pounds)
- Scallions (11)
- Snow peas (8 ounces)
- Spring greens, 1 (9-ounce) bag
- Tomatoes, cherry (1 pint)

Ninja® Foodi™ Digital Air Fry Oven
CHARTS

Air Fry Cooking Chart

INGREDIENT	AMOUNT	PREPARATION	OIL	TEMP	COOK TIME
FROZEN FOOD					
Chicken nuggets	2 boxes (24 oz)	None	None	400°F	26–30 mins
Fish fillets (breaded)	1 package (10 fillets)	None	None	400°F	16–18 mins
Fish sticks	1 box (16 oz)	None	None	400°F	14–16 mins
French fries	16 oz	None	None	390°F	28–30 mins
Mozzarella sticks	2 boxes (16 oz)	None	None	375°F	12–15 mins
Pizza rolls	1 bag (24.8 oz, 50 count)	None	None	375°F	11–13 mins
Popcorn shrimp	1 box (16 oz)	None	None	390°F	10–15 mins
Pot stickers	3 bags (30 count)	None	Toss with 1 Tbsp canola oil	390°F	18–20 mins
Tater tots	2 lbs	None	None	360°F	20-25 mins

INGREDIENT	AMOUNT	PREPARATION	OIL	TEMP	COOK TIME
MEAT, POULTRY, FISH					
Bacon	½ package (8 oz)	None	None	390°F	7–10 mins
Burgers	5¼-lb patties, 80% lean	1 inch thick	None	375°F	10–12 mins
Chicken drumsticks	6 drumsticks	Pat dry	Brush with oil	400°F	22–35 mins
Chicken thighs	5 thighs (4–6 oz each)	Pat dry	Brush with oil	390°F	22–28 mins
Chicken wings	2 lbs	Pat dry	1 Tbsp	400°F	28–30 mins
Crab cakes	6 cakes (6–8 oz each)	None	Brush with oil	390°F	15–18 mins
Salmon fillets	5 fillets (6–8 oz each)	None	Brush with oil	390°F	18–20 mins
Sausage	12 sausages, whole	None	None	390°F	12–14 mins
Shrimp	2 lbs	Pat dry	None	390°F	7–10 mins

INGREDIENT	AMOUNT	PREPARATION	OIL	TEMP	COOK TIME
VEGETABLES					
Asparagus	2 bunches	Cut in half, trim stems	2 Tbsp	420°F	12–15 mins
Beets	1½ lbs	Peel, cut in ½-inch cubes	1 Tbsp	390°F	28–30 mins
Bell peppers (for roasting)	4 peppers	Cut in quarters, remove seeds	1 Tbsp	400°F	15–20 mins
Broccoli	1 large head	Cut in 1–2-inch florets	1 Tbsp	400°F	15–20 mins
Brussels sprouts	1 lb	Cut in half, remove stems	1 Tbsp	425°F	15–20 mins
Carrots	1 lb	Peel, cut in ¼-inch rounds	1 Tbsp	425°F	10–15 mins
Cauliflower	1 head	Cut in 1–2-inch florets	2 Tbsp	400°F	20–22 mins
Corn on the cob	7 ears	Whole ears, remove husks	1 Tbps	400°F	14–17 mins

INGREDIENT	AMOUNT	PREPARATION	OIL	TEMP	COOK TIME
Green beans	1 bag (12 oz)	Trim	1 Tbsp	420°F	18–20 mins
Kale (for chips)	4 oz	Tear into pieces, remove stems	None	325°F	5–8 mins
Mushrooms	16 oz	Rinse, slice thinly	1 Tbsp	390°F	25–30 mins
Potatoes, russet	1½ lbs	Cut in 1-inch wedges	1 Tbsp	390°F	25–30 mins
Potatoes, russet	1 lb	Hand-cut fries, soak 30 mins in cold water, then pat dry	½–3 Tbsp	400°F	25–28 mins
Potatoes, sweet	1 lb	Hand-cut fries, soak 30 mins in cold water, then pat dry	1 Tbsp	400°F	25–28 mins
Zucchini	1 lb	Cut in eighths lengthwise, then cut in half	1 Tbsp	400°F	15–20 mins

Dehydrate Chart

INGREDIENT	AMOUNT	TEMP	TIME
FRUITS & VEGETABLES			
Apples	Cut in ⅛-inch slices, remove core, rinse in lemon water, pat dry	135°F	7–8 hrs
Asparagus	Cut in 1-inch pieces, blanch	135°F	6–8 hrs
Bananas	Peel, cut in ⅜-inch slices	135°F	8–10 hrs
Beets	Peel, cut in ⅛-inch slices	135°F	7–8 hrs
Eggplant	Peel, cut in ¼-inch slices, blanch	135°F	6–8 hrs
Fresh herbs	Rinse, pat dry, remove stems	135°F	4–6 hrs
Ginger root	Cut in ⅜-inch slices	135°F	6 hrs
Mangos	Peel, cut in ⅜-inch slices, remove pit	135°F	6–8 hrs
Mushrooms	Cleaned with soft brush (do not wash)	135°F	6–8 hrs
Pineapple	Peel, cut in ⅜–½-inch slices, remove core	135°F	6–8 hrs
Strawberries	Cut in half or in ½-inch slices	135°F	6–8 hrs
Tomatoes	Cut in ⅜-inch slices or grate; steam if planning to rehydrate	135°F	6–8 hrs

INGREDIENT	AMOUNT	TEMP	TIME
MEAT, POULTRY, FISH			
Beef jerky	Cut in ¼-inch slices, remove all fat, marinate 8–24 hours	150°F	5–7 hrs
Chicken jerky	Cut in ¼-inch slices, marinate overnight	150°F	5–7 hrs
Salmon jerky	Cut in ¼-inch slices, marinate overnight	150°F	5–7 hrs
Turkey jerky	Cut in ¼-inch slices, marinate overnight	150°F	5–8 hrs

MEASUREMENT CONVERSIONS

VOLUME EQUIVALENTS (LIQUID)

US Standard	US Standard (ounces)	Metric (approximate)
2 tablespoons	1 fl. oz.	30 mL
¼ cup	2 fl. oz.	60 mL
½ cup	4 fl. oz.	120 mL
1 cup	8 fl. oz.	240 mL
1½ cups	12 fl. oz.	355 mL
2 cups or 1 pint	16 fl. oz.	475 mL
4 cups or 1 quart	32 fl. oz.	1 L
1 gallon	128 fl. oz.	4 L

OVEN TEMPERATURES

Fahrenheit (F)	Celsius (C) (approximate)
250°F	120°C
300°F	150°C
325°F	165°C
350°F	180°C
375°F	190°C
400°F	200°C
425°F	220°C
450°F	230°C

VOLUME EQUIVALENTS (DRY)

US Standard	Metric (approximate)
⅛ teaspoon	0.5 mL
¼ teaspoon	1 mL
½ teaspoon	2 mL
¾ teaspoon	4 mL
1 teaspoon	5 mL
1 tablespoon	15 mL
¼ cup	59 mL
⅓ cup	79 mL
½ cup	118 mL
⅔ cup	156 mL
¾ cup	177 mL
1 cup	235 mL
2 cups or 1 pint	475 mL
3 cups	700 mL
4 cups or 1 quart	1 L

WEIGHT EQUIVALENTS

US Standard	Metric (approximate)
½ ounce	15 g
1 ounce	30 g
2 ounces	60 g
4 ounces	115 g
8 ounces	225 g
12 ounces	340 g
16 ounces or 1 pound	455 g

INDEX

ACKNOWLEDGMENTS

Thanks to everyone at Callisto Media, especially Bridget Fitzgerald, Elizabeth Castoria, and Julie Kerr. Thanks, too, to Kenzie Swanhart, Meg Jordan, and Sam Ferguson at Ninja.

ABOUT THE AUTHOR

 JANET A. ZIMMERMAN is the award-winning author of six previous cookbooks, including the bestselling *Instant Pot Obsession*. She writes and cooks with her partner, Dave, in Atlanta.

CPSIA information can be obtained
at www.ICGtesting.com
Printed in the USA
JSHW021750020820
7005JS00002B/2

9 781646 110179